STRATEGY FOR LABOR

STRATEGY FOR LABOR

A Radical Proposal

BY ANDRÉ GORZ

Translated from the French by
Martin A. Nicolaus and Victoria Ortiz

BEACON PRESS BOSTON

First published in France by Éditions du Seuil
under the title *Stratégie Ouvrière et Néocapitalisme*

First published by Beacon Press in 1967

First published as a Beacon Paperback in 1968

Published simultaneously in Canada by
Saunders of Toronto, Ltd.

Beacon Press books are published under the auspices
of the Unitarian Universalist Association

Printed in the United States of America

International Standard Book Number: 0–8070–0597–5

9 8 7 6 5

Translators' Note

THE TRANSLATORS would like to thank Mr. Jean Beaupertuis of St. Pierre et Miquelon, North America, for his invaluable assistance in finding English equivalents for many of the technical economic terms used in this book.

Preface to This Edition

"BECAUSE IT HAS FAILED to engage itself with the problems that dog us during our working days and haunt our dreams at night, politics has not engaged the best of us, or at least the best in us. If people seem complacent or inert, the cause may lie less in them than in a political system that evades and confuses the real issues rather than sharpening or resolving them."

These words of James MacGregor Burns[1] apply to all advanced capitalist countries, whatever their history. In all of them, democracy has grown into a representative system whose main characteristic is not to be representative of any popular will.

The so-called representatives of the people are picked by parties that, far from expressing any popular will, are bureaucratized machines, bent on exerting power on behalf of the "elite" that actually wields that power, and on winning privileges for those who serve the interests of the elite. Parties compete for governmental and administrative posts; they don't set forth competing policies and visions showing how to solve the basic problems of the present and to shape the future.

The people do not have the choice between two (or several) fundamentally distinct sets of policies or programs; their choice is only to have one of several sets of politicians apply policies which, except for some marginal differences, are basically the same.

How has this situation arisen? It springs from the concentration of power in the hands of a small number of private corporations whose decisions have a national and even an international scope. No government can afford to antagonize Big Business, unless its clear resolve is to wage a long, drawn-out battle, appealing to mass mobilization and active popular support, with the aim of transferring economic power to the public (which may

[1] In *The Deadlock of Democracy: Four-Party Politics in America*, Englewood Cliffs: Prentice-Hall, Inc. (1963), p. 1.

mean the State, but does not necessarily do so). In the absence of public pressure in this direction, government must bend to the interests of Big Business and toe the latter's line. It must keep Big Business prosperous or the whole nation will suffer from the corporations' ill will, and so will the government's popularity. The prosperity of Big Business depends on constant State intervention to keep the profit rates attractive and investment booming. In the guise of bringing corporate interests into line with the general interest, the general interest, conversely, must be brought into line with the interest of Big Business.

This constant mutual adjustment of business and governmental policies explains the strengthening of the power wielded by the State, and the weakening of the influence held by representative assemblies. Such "serious matters" as the military budget, the rate and the taxation of profits, the use to be made of the economic surplus, the volume and the location of new investments, diplomatic or military intervention abroad, must not be discussed by "irresponsible" delegates of the people, since these might question rather than understand and cooperate with the leading corporations' aims.

Thus, the nation becomes identified with the policies of its leading firms; the foremost task of the State is to protect and to coordinate the latters' interests. Effective power, as Eisenhower once said, belongs to the "military-industrial complex." The monopoly of decision making and of information lies with the bureaucracies of the leading corporations and of the State. Modern capitalism has thus evolved a system of domination in which people have no democratic control over their political parties, their elected assemblies, or their labor unions; in which "democracy" is but a method of manipulating the atomized masses into accepting decisions they do not share in making, of preventing citizens from organizing themselves, from shaping, expressing, and exerting their will collectively.

We have no power over what to produce, how to produce it, or for what market to produce; we have no power over what needs or whose needs are to be given priority. We are hardly able to define our own needs, since the chances to discuss them publicly and freely are scarce. We have no power over the social and technical division of labor, no power over the decisions of the monopolies or of the State which shape our daily existence and the surroundings in which we live. What is left? The so-called basic freedoms, but even these are in jeopardy when real power is so concentrated and thus narrows the field in which self-determination may prevail.

Must we then consider the more or less gentle authoritarianism of the modern State as a foolproof system of domination? Or does affluent capitalism produce situations, men, and needs that tend to subvert its logic?

The author's reply is that capitalist affluence clearly gives rise to needs that it cannot satisfy and that may assume an explosive character. What is meant are not the needs of the old or of the new poor, which comprise one fifth of the population of Western Europe as well as of the United States. Poverty as such never was and cannot be the driving force in the struggle for social change and liberation. It can become such a force only if the poor act not as underprivileged individuals, each looking for help from above (from the State, the wealthy, the welfare institutions), but as a cohesive group or community bent on winning the right of self-government, the power of changing a society that denies recognition to their needs.

The poor of affluent societies are not ordinarily representative of their class. Social origin, education, race, age, geography, etc., divide them. They are in no condition to organize themselves into cohesive groups. But less poor sectors of the population can organize—all those who work manually or intellectually as actual or potential groups, in the factories, offices, or universities. Modern technology and civilization have created new needs in them. These needs, however, are no longer mainly quantitative ones; they tend to become qualitative; they are mainly the need to find some satisfaction and some meaning in the work being done, which generally calls for a higher degree of education, training, and responsibility than in the past, yet without carrying any higher degree of self-determination as to the aims and the ways of working.

These qualitative needs are not easily perceived. They are far less immediate than pain or hunger. As forcefully shown by Herbert Marcuse,[2] they can be repressed and blurred by propaganda, indoctrination, and fun into some vague feeling of dissatisfaction and emptiness. They have no spontaneous means of self-expression. Hunger calls for food to eat. But what does emptiness, boredom, dissatisfaction with life and with the world call for? There is no predetermined answer to this question; we have reached a stage where needs could be no longer those of the "human animal," but those—potentially creative—of the "human man." As manifestations of man's (however partial) emancipation from nature, they could be one and the same as freedom, that is, needs for self-fulfillment and self-determination within work and leisure, of reconciliation between social and individual existence. They could be, but this possibility is not automatically perceived; the very existence of "free needs" depends on the social individual's ability to win consciousness of his potential freedom. It is this ability, as Herbert Marcuse emphasized, which is counteracted and repressed by affluent capitalism's methods of domination.

This is why empirical sociologists tend to question the existence of these new and higher needs. The empirical individual is so conditioned by social and cultural patterns, by indoctrination, values, and ways of reasoning that he cannot generally formulate what he feels. Public opinion and prevailing ideologies are usually well behind real situations and tend to prevent people from grasping them. Becoming conscious of how things really are and of the possibilities they offer never was a spontaneous process but the arduous achievement of avant-garde minorities or visionaries. This is truer nowadays than ever before. To reveal deeply felt (but also hidden) needs and articulate them, we first must show how their satisfaction is actually within our reach; that, for instance, repetitive work, regimentation at the places of work, and authoritarian division of labor are no longer technical necessities and can be fought against successfully; that squalor, ignorance,

[2] In *One-Dimensional Man*, Boston: Beacon Press (1964).

insecurity, new scarcities coexisting with waste, etc., can be done away with; and that a system that makes people work like zombies to produce useless, destructive, or self-destructive things has outlived its usefulness.

This demonstration is being carried out with great vigor in some sections of the European working class movement. It is a practical demonstration, resting on positive counter-propositions and initiative from below as a first step in the direction of collective self-rule. It was initiated in the late fifties in Italy, when a new generation of Communist and socialist labor leaders reestablished democracy within local unions, on the shop floor, and had the workers discuss freely their conditions of work, their grievances, their needs, and the claims they were ready to go on strike for and that were not related to higher wages only.

The wave of labor struggles that ensued was (and still is) an unprecedented experiment in collective self-education. It may be worth noting that some of the leading theoreticians in this experiment drew some inspiration from the struggles waged by the American working class in the last thirty-five years. What is at work in experiments like these is more than just labor tactics or the instant improvement of the worker's lot. What is at work is the establishment of an industrial democracy adapted to conditions in which representative democracy reveals more clearly than ever its inherent limitations. Labor unions and labor action are seen as one of the main instruments (democratic political parties with an overall vision being another prerequisite) for the conquest of popular centers of power and the democratic self-rule from below, on which democracy will have to rest if it is to survive or to be reborn. It will be able to do neither if basic issues remain beyond the reach of those who are most directly concerned by them.

A.G.

Contents

PART TWO: THE LABOR MOVEMENT AND THE COMMON MARKET

PART ONE

Toward an Aggressive Strategy

Introduction

That socialism is a necessity has never struck the masses with the compelling force of a flash of lightning. There has never been direct transition from primitive revolt to the conscious will to change society. Discontent with their condition has never spontaneously led even the most organized workers to attack those structures of society which made their lives unbearable. In this regard, nothing has changed since Lenin, Marx, or Pécqueur.[1]

What has changed, however, is that in the advanced countries the revolt against society has lost its *natural base*. As long as misery, the lack of basic necessities, was the condition of the majority, the need for a revolution could be regarded as obvious. Destitute proletarians and peasants did not need to have a model of a future society in mind in order to rise up against the existing order: the worst was here and now; they had nothing to lose. But conditions have changed since then. Nowadays, in the richer societies, it is not so clear that the status quo represents the greatest possible evil.

Permanent misery still exists, but in France as in the United States, this is the condition of only a fifth of the population. This population, moreover, is not homogeneous. It is concentrated in certain regions and in certain strata which are not representative of their class: for example, among small peasants in isolated regions, the aged, the unemployed, unskilled laborers, etc. These strata are incapable of organizing themselves for decisive action against society and the State. They have the same needs, but no common point of view on how these needs should be satisfied.

This is one reason why poverty can no longer be the basis of the struggle for socialism.

[1] Constantin Pécqueur (1801–1887), a French economist and political theorist who had some influence on the revolutionary movement of 1848. Influenced by utopian socialists, he opposed private property, advocated collectivism, and stressed historical necessity in economic development. [Publisher's note.]

There is a second reason: the workers whose vital needs are insufficiently satisfied are for all practical purposes a rear guard. Advanced capitalism needs skilled workers more than the unskilled, and it also needs consumers for its products. While it is still necessary to demand the satisfaction of immediate needs, this struggle no longer brings the entire social order into radical question.

That is why I will not dwell on misery as the basis for a challenge to capitalism. I will, rather, attempt to determine what new needs capitalist development creates; to determine to what extent these new needs, when we have gauged their depth, are comparable in their urgency to the old needs; and to what extent they too imply a radical critique of capitalism, that is to say a critique of the reasons why these needs remain permanently unsatisfied.

Thus the essential problem will be to determine in which needs the necessity for socialism is rooted now that the urgency born of poverty is blunted; and under what conditions these needs can lead to the consciousness that society must be radically transformed.

This line of thought necessarily leads one to question numerous aspects of the traditional strategy of the working class movement. Not those who question it, however, but reality itself has made that strategy obsolete. In the developed societies, where the pressure of vital needs is attenuated, it is no longer possible to base the necessity for socialism on an immediate negation, rejection, of the status quo. Because the intolerability of this system is no longer absolute, but relative, supplementary mediations are necessary to make the intolerability felt. And these mediations must be *positive:* they must reveal the urgency of the qualitative needs which neo-capitalist ideology ignores or represses; they must make these needs conscious by demonstrating the possibility and the positive conditions of their satisfaction.

It is no longer enough to reason as if socialism were a self-evident necessity. This necessity will no longer be recognized unless the socialist movement specifies what socialism can bring, what problems it alone is capable of solving, and how. Now more than ever it is necessary to present not only an overall alternative but also those "intermediate objectives" (mediations) which lead to it and foreshadow it in the present.

The weakness of the working class and socialist movement in all capitalist countries and particularly in France has up to the present been its more or less pronounced inability to link the struggle for socialism to the everyday demands of the workers. This inability is rooted in historical circumstances. For at least the past thirty years, the Communist movement has propagated the prophecy that capitalism would inevitably, catastrophically collapse. In the capitalist countries, its policy has been to "wait for the revolution." The internal contradictions of capitalism were supposed to sharpen, the condition of the toiling masses to worsen. Inevitably the working class would rise up.

This period has left deep marks. Working class leaders continue to fear that too great a victory in their everyday struggles will remove—or blunt for a long time—the workers' discontent and their revolutionary spirit. These leaders fear that a tangible amelioration in the workers' condition, or a partial victory within the capitalist framework, will reinforce the system and render it more bearable.

These fears, nevertheless, only reflect fossilized thinking, a lack of strategy and theoretical reflection. On the assumption that partial victories within the system would inevitably be absorbed by it, an impenetrable barrier has been erected between present struggles and the future socialist solution. The road from one to the other has been cut. These leaders act as if the solution to all problems could wait until the working class had seized power, and as if in the meantime there were nothing to do but to stoke the flames of revolutionary discontent.

However, this kind of attitude leads to an impasse. Lacking perspectives and positive accomplishments, the revolutionary flame begins to dim. Certainly, capitalism is incapable of fundamentally resolving the essential problems which its development has brought about. But capitalism can resolve these in its own way, by means of concessions and superficial repairs aimed at making the system socially tolerable. At present the working class and socialist movement finds itself cornered and on the defensive: having failed to impose its own solutions, it has lost the initiative. Having failed to anticipate the foreseeable problems and to define the solutions beforehand, the working class ceases to assert itself as the potential ruling class. Quite the contrary, it is capitalism itself which then grants the workers half-solutions. And with each of these concessions, capitalism—left at liberty to define for itself the nature and scope of its measures—strengthens its lead and consolidates its power.

This is also true of the problems arising from the Common Market, of the imbalances and disparities between regions, of the problems of reconversion, development, economic planning, job-creation, training, and professional adaptation to technological evolution. Capitalism does not have a solution to any of these problems, much less a satisfactory solution. But the European labor movement (with the exception, sometimes, of the Italian) has not yet been able to define its own solutions concretely and to fight for them. This is why the movement has hardly advanced at all toward the seizure of power and has not increased in strength. That also is why the movement does not convince those who are not already convinced that, once in power, it will be able to offer a fundamental solution to all problems. The movement behaves as though the question of power were resolved: "Once we're in power . . ." But the whole question is precisely to get there, to create the means and the will to get there.

Is it possible *from within*—that is to say, without having previously destroyed capitalism—to impose anti-capitalist solutions which will not immediately be incorporated into and subordinated to the system? This is the old question of "reform or revolution." This was (or is) a paramount question when the movement had (or has) the choice between a struggle for reforms and armed insurrection. Such is no longer the case in Western Europe; here there is no longer an alternative. The question here revolves around the possibility of "revolutionary reforms," that is to say, of reforms which advance toward a radical transformation of society. Is this possible?

Straight off we must rule out the nominalist objection. All struggle for reform is not necessarily reformist. The not always very clear dividing line between reformist reforms and non-reformist reforms can be defined as follows:

A reformist reform is one which subordinates its objectives to the criteria of rationality and practicability of a given system and policy. Reformism rejects those objectives and demands—however deep the need for them—which are incompatible with the preservation of the system.

On the other hand, a not necessarily reformist reform is one which is conceived not in terms of what is possible within the framework of a given system and administration, but in view of what should be made possible in terms of human needs and demands.

In other words, a struggle for non-reformist reforms—for anti-capitalist reforms—is one which does not base its validity and its right to exist on capitalist needs, criteria, and rationales.[2] A non-

[2] The "counter-plan," i.e., an alternative plan (see also p. 61 *infra*) advocated in France by a minority of socialists, is an ambiguous notion. French Communists criticize its reformism. It is impossible to decide *a priori* if this criticism is well founded or not.

At least as it was presented in a pamphlet entitled "In Favor of a Workers' Front" (*Pour un front des travailleurs*, by *Cercle Les Voix du Socialisme*, Editions Julliard, 1963), the counter-plan program begins by defining objectives in terms of needs, then determining under what conditions and on what terms the objectives can be attained.

Is it reformist, for example, to demand the construction of 500,000 new housing units a year, or a real democratization of secondary and higher education? It is impossible to know beforehand. One would have to decide first whether the proposed housing program would mean the expropriation of those who own the required land, and whether the construction would be a socialized public service, thus destroying an important center of the accumulation of private capital; or if, on the contrary, this would mean subsidizing private enterprise with taxpayers' money to guarantee its profits.

One must also know whether the intention is to build workers' housing anywhere that land and materials can be cheaply bought, or if it is to construct lodgings as well as new industry according to optimum human and social criteria.

Depending on the case, the proposal of 500,000 housing units will be either neo-capitalist or anti-capitalist.

reformist reform is determined not in terms of what can be, but what should be. And finally, it bases the possibility of attaining its objective on the implementation of fundamental political and economic changes. These changes can be sudden, just as they can be gradual. But in any case they assume a modification of the relations of power; they assume that the workers will take over powers or assert a force (that is to say, a non-institutionalized force) strong enough to establish, maintain, and expand those tendencies within the system which serve to weaken capitalism and to shake its joints. They assume structural reforms.[3]

Nevertheless, is it not inevitable that powers gained by the workers within the capitalist framework be reabsorbed by the system and subordinated to its functioning? This question is essential for the Marxist movement, and the only possible answer (which is the answer of the great majority of Italian Marxists, whether Communists or, such as Lelio Basso and Vittorio Foa, left wing Socialists) is the following: the risk of subordination exists, but subordination *is not inevitable*. The risk must be run, for there is no other way. Seizure of power by insurrection is out of the question, and the waiting game leads the workers' movement to disintegration. The only possible line for the movement is to seize, from the present on, those powers which will prepare it to assume the leadership of society and which will permit it in the meantime to control and to plan the development of the society, and to establish certain limiting mechanisms which will restrict or dislocate the power of capital.

[3] Each time I use the term structural reform, it should be understood that this does not mean a reform which rationalizes the existing system while leaving intact the existing distribution of powers; this does not mean to delegate to the (capitalist) State the task of improving the system.

Structural reform is by definition a reform implemented or controlled by those who demand it. Be it in agriculture, the university, property relations, the region, the administration, the economy, etc., a structural reform *always* requires the creation of new centers of democratic power.

Whether it be at the level of companies, schools, municipalities, regions, or of the national Plan, etc., structural reform always requires a *decentralization* of the decision making power, a *restriction on the powers of State or Capital*, an *extension of popular power*, that is to say, a victory of democracy over the dictatorship of profit. No nationalization is *in itself* a structural reform.

It is not, therefore, the opportuneness of "counter-powers" which is in question, but their nature and their relationship to the power of the capitalist State. The alternative is not between the conquest, exercise, and constant enlargement of powers by the workers, on the one hand, and the necessarily abstract will to seize power, on the other. The choice is between subordinate powers and autonomous powers.

By subordinate powers must be understood the association or participation of workers in an economic policy which urges them to share the responsibility on the level of results and execution, while at the same time it forbids them to become involved in the decisions and the criteria according to which this policy has been decreed. For example, the union is invited to "participate" in a policy predetermined by others on the company level[4] and to "share" in carrying out this policy. The union is permitted to "challenge" the implementation, or even the effects of capitalist administration. But it is hoped at the same time that it will in fact not be able to challenge the *effects*, since it has been made an accomplice to the premises from which they follow. And as an additional precaution, management provides for an "arbitrator" to make sure that the challenge to the effects does not place these premises in question.

By *autonomous* power, on the other hand, must be understood the power of the workers to challenge, in opposing the effects and the methods of implementation, the very premises of the management's policy; to challenge them even in anticipation, because they control all the particulars on the basis of which the management's policy is elaborated. We shall return to this at greater length later on. Such autonomous power is a first step toward the subordination of the exigencies of production to human exigencies, with the conquest of the power of autonomous control as an ultimate goal.

The exercise of this kind of autonomous power cannot be restricted to purely negative opposition. But it is also clear that this power will never be granted, nor even conceded, by the employers without a struggle.[5] This power must be won by force.

[4] Cf. François Bloch-Laîné, *Pour une réforme de l'entreprise* (Coll. *L'Histoire immédiate*), Éditions du Seuil, 1963.

And even when it is won (as in the case of the Italian metal workers, after nine months of struggle, May 1962 to February 1963), this power can be exercised only at the price of constant mobilization. Moreover, it will inevitably tend to extend beyond the framework of the large enterprise, because the policy of a monopoly or of an oligopoly is in such close reciprocal relation with the economic policies of the State, the life of the city, the community, and the region.[6]

Far, then, from leading toward the integration and subordination of the labor movement to the State, the autonomous power of the workers—in the large enterprises, but also in the cities, the towns, public services, regional bodies, cooperatives, etc.—prepares the way for a dialectical progression of the struggle to a higher and higher level. Autonomous power is at once the generator and the indispensable relay station for the elaboration and pursuit of the integral objectives of a policy aimed at replacing capitalism.

Moreover, this autonomous power is an indispensable element in the training and education of the masses, making it possible for them to see socialism not as something in the transcendental beyond, in an indefinite future, but as the visible goal of a praxis already at work; not a goal which the masses are supposed to wish for abstractly, but one to aim for by means of partial objectives in which it is foreshadowed.

What is involved here is indeed a strategy of *progressive* conquest of power by the workers, a strategy which does not, how-

[5] "The union's contractual power in the shop is only accepted by the employers while it is *apparent*—that is to say, while it participates in a predetermined and centralized policy—but not while it becomes real, that is to say when it expresses the real demands of the workers with regard to the real conditions of their work." Vittorio Foa, assistant secretary of the CGIL, in *Rassegna sindacale*, 28 September 1963, a biweekly publication of Editríci Sindacale Italiana, Rome.

[6] The Italian General Confederation of Labor (CGIL—*Confederazione Generale Italiana del Lavoro*) and—partly, at least—the French Confederation of Christian Workers (CFTC—*Confédération Française des Travailleurs Chrétiens*) consider the union's power to control and to influence the management of big businesses as the primary condition of anti-monopolist or democratic planning. (For further information, see the Appendix.)

ever, exclude the possibility of or even the necessity for a revolutionary seizure of power at a later stage.

Is such a strategy a step backward, because it abandons the idea of seizing power right away, of installing socialism with one blow? That would be the case if a revolutionary seizure of power were possible, or if the preparation for this seizure maintained the masses in a state of mobilization. But such is not the case. It is impossible—above all for Marxists—to pretend to explain the masses' present state of demobilization by the absence of revolutionary fervor on the part of their leaders. In truth, the state of demobilization today is due to the fact that neither the possibility nor the form nor the content of the workers' potential political power has been defined.

As long as the condition of the workers was immediately and absolutely unbearable, the conquest of power was an immediate end in itself. At present, however, the conquest of power is not a goal which will gain support unless it is made clear toward what ends—unrealizable under capitalism—the workers' power will be *the means*. Why socialism? How will it be achieved?

The answer to these questions is today a necessary first step. Mobilization for the conquest of power and of socialism—abstract terms which no longer in themselves serve to mobilize the masses—must pass through the "mediation" of intermediate, mobilizing objectives. The struggle for partial objectives which arise from deep needs and bring into question the capitalist structure, the struggle for partial autonomous powers and their exercise should present socialism to the masses as a living reality already at work, a reality which attacks capitalism from within and which struggles for its own free development. Instead of dichotomizing the future and the present—future power and present impotence, like Good and Evil—what must be done is to bring the future into the present, to make power tangible *now* by means of actions which demonstrate to the workers their positive strength, their ability to measure themselves against the power of capital and to impose their will on it.

Certainly, socialism can be no less than the hegemony of the working class, the public ownership of the means of production.

But in order to reach this goal, it is necessary first to aim at intermediate objectives by means of which socialism can be seen as possible, as having a concrete significance, as being within reach. If socialism is to result from the prolongation of the present day struggles and demands, it cannot be presented straight off as a whole system, as a solution which precedes all problems. It should be presented instead as the general direction in which concrete solutions to specific problems move. In this respect, nationalization, like power, is no longer today, as in the days of Pécqueur, an end in itself: to achieve it there must be a struggle, but before there can be a struggle it must first be clear toward what end nationalization is the means.[7]

Politically, socialism can mean no less than power to the working class; economically, it can mean nothing but collective ownership of the means of production, that is to say the end of exploitation. But socialism is also more than that: it is also a new type of relationship among men, a new order of priorities, a new model of life and of culture. If it is not all this also, it loses its meaning. This meaning, to define it in one sentence, is: the subordination of production to needs, as much for *what* is produced as for *how* it is produced. It is understood that in a developed society, needs are not only quantitative: the need for consumer goods; but also qualitative: the need for a free and many-sided development of human faculties; the need for information, for communication, for

[7] Nationalization of the steel industry, for example, which was once a political aim, is today the least interesting of the foreseeable nationalizations, for this ancient industry is losing speed, its profitability is low, and it is already virtually controlled by the State. Nationalization, instead of changing the power relations and opening a breach in the capitalist system, can also strengthen this system: a neo-capitalist government, in purchasing the steel industry, could render a service to its present owners by permitting them to invest their capital much more profitably in growing industries.

The aim must rather be to nationalize the latter, the principal centers of capital accumulation, such as the chemical, oil, electronic, and mechanical and electrical construction industries; for the workers in these industries—including the technicians—suffer the consequences of the anarchic way they are run.

fellowship; the need to be free not only from exploitation but from oppression and alienation in work and in leisure.

If in the first two chapters which follow we deal more with labor union strategy than with political strategy, this is because the union, much more than the party, is the body in which class consciousness in a neo-capitalist society is catalyzed and elaborated. In fact, in all its aspects, neo-capitalist civilization tends to be a mass civilization. Its propaganda, which is above all commercial, subordinates the means which individuals have for informing themselves and for being in touch with one another, to commercial criteria. In order to sell newspapers, radio time, or products of mass consumption, capitalist civilization aims at the common and average characteristics in men, seeking to efface and mask the conflicts which oppose them to each other and the barriers which separate them: the big brands, the big corporation, the big press must gain the favor of a heterogeneous and varied public. They will therefore ignore everything which divides and differentiates this public, conjure away the burning problems which confront it, and address it as a mass of "consumers" above class frontiers. The negation of classes is an ideology founded on mercantilism.

It is normal that this ideology, the carrier of "mass culture," should invade the public domain, and that political parties (or rather, men) seeking clients should appropriate the mass ideology and its methods of commercial seduction. It is even more normal that monopoly- and state-capitalism should work toward the concentration and continuity of power,[8] and that, once the presidential regime is in place, the political parties are forced to regroup in two camps in their competition for supreme power.

"Mass culture" tends thus to be followed by "mass democracy," that is to say the competition of all groups for the support of the "center," of the "masses," of those least politicized. Thus, during an electoral or pre-electoral period, the two camps take

[8] The question to what extent this is inherent in all industrially advanced societies will be discussed later.

turns in smoothing the edges, attenuating the conflicts, divisions, and differences.

Union autonomy, then, assumes prime importance. For the labor union becomes the only mass organization to escape the imperatives of mass democracy; far from becoming weaker, it is reinforced as it reveals the true concreteness of problems. In the factory, the community, and the region, the union becomes the only place where class consciousness—the consciousness of needs, of demands, and of ends to be pursued—are elaborated, the sanctuary where the conflict between labor and capital continues to be experienced in all its sharpness. The union struggle inevitably assumes a political context, because the link between the workers' condition on the job and the organization of society, between the specific demands of the workers and the economic, political, and social conditions necessary to satisfy them, is so evident.

That is why we must firmly reject all attempts to subordinate the union to the party, to limit or discipline the union's autonomy of action, to submit its action to objective criteria such as economic fluctuations, the evolution of productivity, of production, or of profits. This firm defense of the union's freedom of action must be unconditional and permanent, no matter what the political color of the government, no matter what type of economic planning there is and what its goals are.

There are three fundamental reasons for this:

1. The first is economic. Although it still has many partisans in Western Europe, an authoritarian wage policy, linking the level of wages to that of productivity, has shown itself to be impracticable wherever it has been attempted, even in socialist countries. In the latter, just as the planners have come to recognize the importance of the market as *indicator* of individual demand—and thus, to a limited degree, as *regulator* of production according to needs—so also have they come to recognize the importance of a "labor market," that is to say, the importance of union autonomy.

In fact, it is impossible to assess the value of labor power according to purely objective, economic criteria.

Such an evaluation could not take into account the attractive or repelling features of different jobs which require equal skills and are equally productive.

Such an evaluation would not make it possible to draw workers to—and keep them in—the jobs and the regions where they are socially needed, but where their productivity increases more slowly than elsewhere.

Such an evaluation would either risk exhausting the manpower available for these jobs, or it would make authoritarian recruitment necessary, a compulsory selection (including the compulsion of unemployment).

Such an evaluation would discourage technical progress in the industries and services with low productivity, for technical progress would not be resolutely pursued unless the rising cost of labor made it necessary for economic reasons.

If we attempt to overcome the inconveniences of a wage policy keyed to the productivity of the different industrial sectors and regions individually, by substituting for it an undifferentiated wage policy keyed no longer to the development of local productivity but to the development of overall productivity, the result will be no better. The latter policy, in fact, would discourage the pursuit of technological progress in the branches of high productivity, which are also the most concentrated branches and those most apt to promote technological research. Freed from union pressure, the oligopolies or monopolies which control these branches would cease to feel the need to make economical use of human labor. They would regulate productivity and thus the living standard of the workers as they saw fit. The most powerful stimulus to technical progress would disappear if the permanent tension between wages and productivity were to disappear, a tension which only the union's freedom of action could maintain.[9]

2. The second reason for categorically rejecting any encroachment on the union's freedom of action is that this freedom has the

[9] On this subject see the excellent study by Paolo Santi, "Sindacati e politiche di controllo dei salari," *Quaderni di Sindacato Moderno* (Rome: FIOM [*Federazione Impiegati e Operai Metallurgici*—the CGIL Metalworkers Union—headed by Bruno Trentin], 1964), I.

permanent function *of expressing the needs arising out of production* and, more broadly, out of social life. The union's role is to challenge the inert exigencies of the production process in the name of the living exigencies of the workers, in order to subordinate the former to the latter. "Wages are the historical price of labor power . . . a price linked to the development of social needs. . . ." The function of wages is not only to bring about changes in the orientation of economic development, but also "to record the average level of needs which these changes have brought about." [10]

Any subordination of the union's freedom of action—that is to say, of the possibility of expressing these needs—to a given economic situation should thus be condemned under normal circumstances as fundamentally anti-democratic.

3. On a political (or political-economic) level, finally, organized union action is the principal means by which the working class movement can bring capitalism to a crisis, by revealing the system's inability, even in highly developed countries, to give priority to the satisfaction of fundamental needs, its inability to initiate and to implement the necessary structural reforms, notably the public direction of investments and public planning of the economy according to real needs. These measures do not become politically possible unless and until pressure from the masses makes it impossible for the system to function according to its own logic.

Even among those who sympathize with socialism, it is often objected that in order to achieve a new economic orientation—for example, democratic or socialist planning—the union should accept as part of the bargain a limit on its freedom of action, a wage discipline. I cannot agree.[11]

The permanent role of the union is to express the workers'

[10] *Ibid.*

[11] Cf. on this subject the position of the CGIL as it was presented at the 14th Congress of the FIOM. See also Bruno Trentin, "Politica dei redditi e programmazione," *Critica Marxista*, a bimonthly theoretical publication of the Italian Communist Party, Via delle Botteghe Oscure 4, Rome, I (1964), especially pp. 54–59.

real needs and to work toward their satisfaction; the role of the national Plan, in whose elaboration the union has every interest in participating, is to organize *the means* for this satisfaction. The tension between the needs and the means to satisfy them is indeed the driving force of economic planning and therefore of democracy. The tension between the union and the Plan should be accepted as a permanent fact.

When union pressure places the objectives of a Plan in danger, it is the latter which must defend itself, and it has the means to do so. To the extent that the union has approved the goals of the Plan—goals which it has to a great degree imposed on the planners—to that extent will it accept the means of defense used by the Plan. These means are essentially fiscal; they will consist, in particular, of absorbing excessive purchasing power which might appear after labor victories by means of direct taxes and specific taxes on consumption. And it goes without saying that the Plan's countermeasures—the nature of the taxes, the orientation and the priorities which they lend to consumption, the expenditures or investments which they must cover—may in their turn be disputed or negotiated by the union.[12]

A national incomes policy is not at all a necessary element in economic planning. The incomes policy merely expresses the political will of organized capitalism to integrate the union into the system, to subordinate consumption to production, and production to the maximization of profit. The union cannot defend itself against this political will except by an opposite and autonomous political will which is independent of party and State, and is rooted in the specific demands of the workers.

Bastion of class realities in the face of mass ideologies and their myths, the union—to the extent that it functions properly—becomes a center which radiates political energy.[13] It is through the

[12] In practice, union wage pressure in a "socializing" or transitional economy would obviously have the effect of constantly reinforcing public initiative to the detriment of private initiative, because of the influence of similar redistributions of the national income in the public interest.

[13] Union action, however, can break through only if the class contradictions which it reveals are translated into a unifying political perspective and

union that the fundamental contradiction of capitalism—the contradiction inherent in property relations—is continually manifest in its concrete, living reality. It is in the union, within the sphere of alienated labor, that the truth and the meaning (if not the immediate content) of revolutionary demands take shape: the demand that production be subordinated to needs, the manner of producing be subjected to the human exigencies of the producers, capital subordinated to society. Only in the union can socialist man be forged in the present: the worker organized with other workers to regulate production and exchange, the producer dominating the production process instead of being subordinated to it, the man of creative praxis. Socialism will be little—or nothing at all—if it is not first these men, if it is not a new order of priorities, a new model of consumption, of culture, of social collaboration.

This model has yet to be defined in any of the advanced industrialized societies. It does not yet exist anywhere. Until now, socialist societies also have subordinated consumption to production; creative needs, culture, and education to the needs of accumulation. This subordination has even been, in certain regards, more systematic and relentless than in the advanced phase of capitalism.

For socialism has until now been no more than a gigantic and systematic effort at public accumulation, impelled by the acute shortage of everything and by external menaces. This is now generally admitted. But above all, the problem is to determine how this wartime socialism, this socialism of scarcity which has little to do with the socialism conceived by Marx, can overcome its alienations and return to its original goals.

For when we begin by considering individuals as means of production, society as an instrument of accumulation, and work as a tool for producing other tools (which is what the socialist states have undeniably done up to now) then we are not preparing men to emancipate themselves and to construct a society in which production is a means and man is the end.

---

struggle by radical parties. Working class parties are powerless in the absence of the laboring masses' struggle, but the latter can get nowhere in the absence of a radical political force.

By subordinating human ends to technical exigencies, the victory over scarcity risks being vitiated. A society which has for too long been the means of, instead of the reason for, production will inevitably grow rigid and fall prey to bureaucratic sclerosis which, in preventing needs from showing themselves, prevents production from adjusting to these needs even when this adjustment becomes theoretically possible, and perverts the concept and the functioning of an economic plan.

In point of fact, even where acute scarcity has been overcome, socialism still exists only as an often malfunctioning infrastructure.[14] There is only one exception: Yugoslavia, where despite scarcity, structures have been established without delay for the purpose of subordinating production to needs, the means to the end—that is to say, to the emancipation and full development of the workers, of man. Particular historical circumstances from which it is impossible to generalize have permitted this exception. (Furthermore, the Yugoslavs have committed the error of not having sufficiently appreciated in their foreign policy the fact that their experience is of an exceptional character.)

But that is not the issue. What I mean to emphasize with this parenthesis is that today there is not and there cannot be a socialist society which the working class movements of the advanced capitalist nations may take as a model. The perspective, the demands of the working class movement in Western Europe can and *must* be more advanced, insofar as the construction of socialism is concerned, than those of the existing socialist societies. The problem of the humanization of production, its subordination to the exigencies and needs of individuals, can be approached in more advanced terms by us than by anyone else. Moreover, that is precisely what the Marxist vanguard of the socialist countries expects of the Marxists of Western Europe.

[14] Notably in Czechoslovakia, economic planning has not prevented the production of immense quantities of goods which were unsalable because they had nothing to do with needs and with taste (to the value of $104 million in 1963).

CHAPTER ONE

Beyond the Paycheck

THERE IS NO CRISIS in the workers' movement, but there is a crisis in the theory of the workers' movement. This crisis (in the sense of reexamination, critique, broadening of strategic thought) arises principally from the fact that immediate economic demands no longer suffice to express and to make concrete the radical antagonism of the working class to capitalism; and that these demands, no matter how hard the struggle for them, are no longer enough to bring capitalist society to the point of crisis, nor to strengthen the autonomy of the working class within the society of which it is a part.

Now, the explicit and positive affirmation of class autonomy is one essential precondition for the attainment of revolutionary perspective in the working class movement. And by class autonomy one must understand first of all that the working class, in its everyday actions as well as in its attitude toward society, considers itself the permanent challenge not only to the capitalist economic system and social order, but also and equally to capitalist power and civilization (its priorities, its value hierarchies, its culture) in the name of a different power and a different civilization of which the working class, as the potential ruling class, makes itself daily the author and the prefiguration.

1. *From Misery to Poverty*

When I say that the struggle over the paycheck no longer suffices to express the fundamental antagonism of the classes, I mean above all that, in the mature capitalist societies, the problems of the standard of living, of wages and of the simple reproduction of labor power no longer possess an urgency great enough to allow one to envisage the overthrow of the system and the end of exploitation as their necessary outcome. For the working class, the intolerability of the capitalist system has become relative, and the overthrow or transformation of that system no longer appears as a clear and vital necessity, as was the case thirty or fifty years ago. As a result, struggles for immediate economic demands, even very bitter ones, no longer by themselves open up perspectives of revolutionary social change; they even accommodate themselves to the most insipid trade-unionist and reformist ideology.

To maintain the theory of absolute impoverishment in these conditions is entirely useless. Not that this theory is absolutely false from the economic point of view. If by absolute impoverishment one means not the decline of the average worker's buying power over a given period,[1] but the growing disparity between buying power on the one hand, and, on the other, the real cost of the social reproduction of labor power under changing conditions of life (and above all the broader reproduction made necessary by technological development and the new skills required as a result, with all that this implies, especially in cultural investment, professional education of the worker and of his children)—then the theory of absolute impoverishment retains some validity.[2] For all that, it has nevertheless changed its meaning.

Originally, the theory of impoverishment meant that there was an immediate, explosive contradiction between the vital needs of the workers and the iron law of a capitalist system which condemned its workers to a workweek of seven days and seventy hours or more, to undernourishment, to early physical exhaustion, etc. It meant that capitalism signified for the worker the impossibility of living and that, inversely, the mere affirmation of the right to live was in itself already a revolutionary negation of the society. To the degree that the society denied to the worker the possibility of reproducing his physical labor power, the mere

[1] The General Confederation of Labor (CGT—*Confédération Générale du Travail*) claimed recently that the workers' buying power had declined by 30% in twenty years in the Paris area. (For further information, see the Appendix.)

[2] Cf. the interpretations of this theory in the works of Arzoumanian, André Barjonet, and Roger Garaudy, who are not in agreement with the thesis that Marx presented in the *1844 Manuscripts*, nor with the thesis, cited above, which the CGT continues to defend.

demand for the most basic consumer needs had an immediately apparent revolutionary content. The necessity for revolution became the same as the necessity of living; its material base was direct and simple.

Now, it is sufficient to examine the latest revivals of the theory of impoverishment to become aware that this theory, now founded on economic reasoning, has lost its immediate and self-evident clarity. While one can with some ingenuity prove that the needs relating to the reproduction of labor power are increasingly unsatisfied, it nevertheless remains true that these needs (historical, and no longer elementary) now do not have an absolutely imperative character. Does this mean that revolution is no longer necessary? That, at least, is what the bourgeois theoreticians of "affluence" argue. And it is in order to refute them that the theoreticians of the French Communist Party (PCF—*Parti Communiste Français*) or of the CGT, clinging to the theory of impoverishment, continually demonstrate that workers have never been poorer, that the range of unsatisfied demands has never been greater. In so doing they bypass the fundamental problem.

In effect, they are right and wrong at the same time. Right, because in a given society at a given level of development the notion of poverty designates the totality of possibilities (notably cultural, sanitary, medical) and of wealth which are denied to an individual while at the same time being held up to him as the norm potentially valid for all. That poverty has never been greater is therefore a demonstrable assertion. But they are wrong, because to this greater poverty there is no corresponding misery; quite the contrary. The needs that are unsatisfied today are of a different nature from those of fifty or one hundred years ago: then, it was a question of unsatisfied elementary needs (misery); today, it is a question of historical needs, or historical-fundamental needs. (We will discuss this further in Chapter Four.) And the latter do not have the same absolutely imperative urgency as the former. They no longer assert the categorical exigency for life, but the infinitely elastic demand for a better life or for "human" life. And if revolution is an immediate necessity when the possibility of living can only be bought at that price, the same cannot be said when what is at stake is the possibility of living better, or differently.

I do not mean to say that one cannot make a revolution for a better or different life. I mean only that the urgency of revolution is no longer given, in this case, in the nature of consumer needs themselves, and that, if the existing dissatisfactions are to acquire a similar urgency, a higher than ever level of consciousness and of theoretical and practical elaboration are necessary. The error of those who have recourse to modernized forms of the theory of impoverishment has been to try to do without this necessary elevation of the level of consciousness and the level of struggle, without the new mediations necessary to lead from immediate dissatisfaction to the conscious will to bring about a radical transformation. This theory has become a crutch: like the theory of the inevitability of catastrophic crises which was current in the Stalinist era, it bases itself on the *growing discontent of the masses* as if that were an absolute impasse toward which capitalism were headed. Convinced that capitalism can only lead from bad to worse, the theory foresees its absolute intolerability. This allows it to dispense with the elaboration of a strategy of progressive conquest of power and of active intervention into capitalist contradictions.

The impasse predicted for capitalism becomes finally the impasse of the revolutionary waiting game. For while the developed capitalist societies, for better or for worse, integrate the struggles of the working classes as one factor amid others in their pursuit of economic equilibrium, the strategy of the working class, on the other hand, deals with the modern tendencies of mature capitalism only imperfectly in its calculations. Accustomed to find the source of its strength in the immediate intolerability of the system, in its "negative negation," the working class is not always conscious of a number of factors: in mature capitalist society the differences between the classes pertain less to the quantity than to the quality of consumption, and the same "model of affluence" is upheld by the sources of public information and education as suitable for all "consumers"; in such a society it is important to oppose the capitalist model itself with a "positive negation," with a model that is essentially qualitative, one which opposes the priorities of the "affluent society" with different and truer priorities; one which opposes less immediate but more profound needs to those induced by capitalist civilization, needs which no amount of consumption can satisfy. In other words, the revolutionary break between the classes is no longer located within the sphere of consumer needs; quite the contrary.

In effect, with its idle productive capacity and its liquid capital searching for outlets, mature capitalism is in a position to oppose the most flexible line of defense precisely to general demands for greater consumption and leisure. It can absorb both nominal wage increases and a reduction in working hours without harming either profits or above all, the power of the monopolies, and without increasing in any way the power of the working class, despite its victories.

Rather, these immediate struggles, precisely because they are general and undifferentiated, become the objective causes of division in the working class. It is useless to present statistical demonstration of the fact that the basic hourly real wages of the metal workers in the Paris area have remained constant or have declined; it is impossible to base a strategic struggle on this fact, because the workers who are paid the basic hourly rates form a declining fraction of those laborers who are paid by the week, and the latter are a declining fraction of the working class. Management ingeniously diversifies the classifications of status, category, and privileges; it multiplies bonuses for non-absenteeism, for productivity, etc., in addition to bonuses paid simply at the whim of the employer. The wage scale varies with the region, the industry, the company within the industry, the profession, and the category. A general demand for a 5 to 10 per cent increase in basic pay can therefore no longer hope to mobilize an important body of professionals and technicians who, in large enterprises where manpower is short, receive a significant part of their salary in the form of bonuses.[3]

[3] The unions quite properly demand the suppression of the various uncontrollable bonuses, and their incorporation into salary. But this demand cannot solve the problem: it presupposes that the problem is already solved. It presupposes that the union is able to bring the various elements of re-

2. *The Impasse*

It is less important now to know whether or not there is impoverishment in the case of workers paid the minimum hourly wage; what is important is to design a strategy which takes account of the demands of workers as various as the manual laborer on the minimum wage, the semi-skilled worker paid by the hour and according to output, the skilled worker paid by the hour and by the job, the technician or employee paid by the month. It is evident that such a strategy must be based much more on the specific problems of the workers' condition in their various establishments, rather than on statistical averages; on a unifying vision of class conflicts—which are concerned principally with the relations of production, of work, and of power—rather than on a relative average impoverishment of workers, an average which hides growing disparities. The necessary diversity of objectives on the level of direct action cannot be unified except on the level of strategic vision.

General and undifferentiated demands for wage increases can no longer furnish the working class with this unifying perspective. Such demands tend on the contrary to divide the relatively privileged workers in the leading industries—to whom management tends to offer guaranteed annual increases and productivity bonuses—from workers without such privileges, particularly those who work for the State. Such demands express less and less the interests of the working class as such, and more and more the interest of a group of underprivileged consumers.[4] These demands

---

muneration, now in the arbitrary hands of management, under the workers' control and within their negotiating power. How can this result be achieved? It is not enough to assert that it is necessary to achieve it. It must be placed at the center of the struggle. It must be translated into objectives around which mobilization can take place. It is therefore necessary to move the emphasis away from general quantitative demands toward demands for greater control. We shall discuss this further in the following chapter.

[4] The adoption by striking workers of the slogan "Charlot, nos sous!" ("Charlie [de Gaulle], our pay!"), which might be suitable to a protest demonstration by war veterans, perfectly expresses this development.

offer to the mass of salaried workers no other perspective than that of increased *individual consumption.* In other words, they place the workers as a class on the tail end of the "consumers' society" and of its ideology; they do not challenge the model of that society, but only the share of the wealth which the society accords to the salaried consumer. They consciously bring into question neither the workers' condition at the place of work, nor the subordination of consumption to production, nor the capitalist relationships of production; not even the more and more important aspect of exploitation which consists—beyond the extraction of surplus value from direct salary—of the diversion and confiscation of productive resources and human labor for frivolous and wasteful ends. Such demands postulate the working class as one more underprivileged, abstractly conceived stratum among others in the population, not as a class. And they are for that reason compatible with the most conservative trade unionism: the sometimes very bitter struggles of the Anglo-Saxon or German unions during the course of the last fifteen years have never given rise to even the slightest revolutionary perspective.

The conclusion to be drawn from this argument is not that struggles over wages are useless; rather, it is that their effectiveness, insofar as mobilization, unification, and education of the working class are concerned, has become very limited. These struggles by themselves, even if they sometimes succeed in creating a crisis within capitalism, nevertheless succeed neither in preventing capitalism from overcoming its difficulties in its own way, nor in preparing the working class sufficiently to outline and to impose its own solutions to the crises it has provoked. On the contrary, the working class runs the risk of provoking a counteroffensive by the governmental technocracy, an attack leveled not only in the economic, but equally in the ideological, social, and political realms; and the working class, because it did not also wage a fight in these spheres, would be unable to respond with the necessary alertness and cohesion.

The classic effect of successful wage struggles by the working class movement is to unleash a rise in prices and to precipitate an inflationary crisis.[5] In other words, management has a tendency to preserve the rate of profit which is menaced by rising wages by means of raising prices; and since the psychological effect of these increases influences all elements of the cost of living (commercial margins, price of services, agricultural products), the share of the national income which is paid out to wage earners has a tendency to stagnate or even to decline. Inflation thus appears as an effective means of defense—even of planned defense—of the profit rate against pressure by the working class; and, unless the structure is changed, an increase in pressure for higher wages is translated into accelerated inflation. The struggle for a general increase in pay thus bears a constantly defensive character and reveals itself to be incapable of effecting a palpably different redistribution of the national income.

It can thus be made clear that structural reforms, including the socialization of the investment function and therefore a new structure of power, are an essential precondition for a real and lasting amelioration of the living standard of the working class. In other words, beginning with the relative ineffectiveness of wage struggles (again underlined by the theory of absolute impoverishment), one hopes to have convinced the workers that the condition of their victory is *political.* But what conclusions follow? Does it follow that union struggles and mass action must remain sterile, that such action can only demonstrate the discontent of the laboring masses and make them conscious of it, while the solution to their problems must await the political victory of the working-class parties? That sometimes seems to be the attitude of the leaders of the workers' movement in France. Mass actions keep within the limits of pure protest; political slogans, general and abstract, are tacked mechanically onto immediate grievances or onto manifestations of discontent. Often, everything takes place as if the specific problems of the working classes—on the level

[5] Unless, on the other hand, the victory of the unions permits capitalism to avoid a classic crisis of over-production by substituting individual consumption for capital investment and exportation as a stimulant to economic activity, as was the case in West Germany during the period 1959–1961.

of the plant, the industry, the sector, the region—must await the overthrow of capitalism, and meanwhile worsen.

The consequence of this line of conduct is that the working class is encouraged to place all its hope in political and parliamentary victories; meanwhile, it is pledged to play a waiting game, to make immediate demands and to agitate without perspective. A revolutionary phraseology (for instance, that the solution of problems must await the political victory of the working-class parties) goes hand in hand with an everyday union policy of a purely trade-unionist style, and, in the political realm, with promises of structural changes for the indefinite future.

Thus there is a complete break between present action and long term structural objectives, between everyday union struggles and the possible outcome of a total transformation of society. As a result of what one really must call a lack of strategy, the wage-struggle itself grinds to a halt, in the absence of content to feed it; or, what is about the same thing, the struggle becomes side-tracked in corporatist disputes and rivalries between various crafts.

3. *A Political Battle*

Having staked everything on the discontent and frustration of the wage earning masses, the working class movement runs the risk of witnessing the fading away of class consciousness itself, and the reduction of the class struggle (precisely in the manner of trade unionism) to a purely economic struggle for a higher standard of living, a struggle against disparities in income and against the "unjust" distribution of the national revenue and of the fruits of expansion. Then what strategy will it oppose to the neo-capitalist suggestion of an incomes policy coordinated among all "social categories"? It cannot rest on the two traditional objections:

1. The imperfections of the statistical data make comparison of salaried and non-salaried incomes materially impossible.

2. An incomes policy would attack the autonomy of the unions, would substitute negotiations at the summit (as in Sweden

and in the Netherlands) for struggles below, and would tend to enclose the working class movement in the exigencies of capitalist logic.

For these objections, justified as they are, do not touch the heart of the problem. So long as the working class movement sees in wage demands almost the only content of union-organized action, while at the same time asserting that the increase in the cost of living and in the profit rate is faster than that of wages, then how can it persist in its rejection of the incomes policy? For large industry as well as for the State, which lives in close symbiosis with it, the necessity to plan investments, amortization, profits, and labor costs for some time ahead is ever more compelling. To arrive at this end, to make the element of labor costs as foreseeable as that of fixed charges, management and government will not hesitate to perfect their statistical apparatus and to add seduction to the pressures and threats aimed at the workers. What will a labor movement centered on wage struggles and on the theory of impoverishment reply to a promise of a 4 to 5 per cent increase in real wages within the framework of an economic "consensus"?

If the movement has not from the beginning denounced the mutilation inflicted on even the highest paid workers by the despotic organization of industrial labor; if it has not taken a position against the gigantic waste of social resources in the framework of monopolist competition; if it has not conclusively and concretely demonstrated that these private investments whose profitability it is supposed to preserve through wage discipline are scandalous not only because they represent the private appropriation of a social product, but also because of their qualitative and geographical orientation; if it has not at the outset proposed a different scale of priorities, a different investment and consumption structure, in short, a different Plan from that of state- and monopoly-capitalism—then on what bases will it fight for the autonomy of the working class, against the planned incomes policy, against the alleged necessity for respecting the celebrated equilibrium of consumption and investment? Will it limit itself to outbidding the offer economically, asserting that 4 to 5 per cent is a ridiculous proposition, that 8 or 9 per cent have to be obtained, but that this goal can only be reached after a political (electoral) victory over the power of the monopolies?

How can one fail to see that the battle against the planned incomes policy has an essentially political character from the beginning, that the stakes are no longer economic or quantitative, but that what is at stake is the fundamental question of democracy, that is, the labor movement's possibility of fighting in its daily actions the capitalist organization of production and of society, in order to achieve a socialist transformation? How can one still believe that it is only, or especially (with quantitative arguments), for a difference of 4 to 5 per cent per year that the working class can be mobilized most effectively in a battle where its role as ruling class is at stake, a battle which cannot be won except by a mobilization of all its moral resources over a long period, by constantly maintaining class consciousness on its highest level?

In a system whose intolerability is no longer absolute, but relative, one cannot make a revolution for a little more well-being any more than one can begin *and win* the political battle for the autonomy of the working class with quantitative arguments about the level of wages. Also, rather than enter battle on the question of percentages, why not rely on the working class's radical rejection of capitalist society on the level (that of the capitalist relations of production) where this rejection is permanently experienced? And why not from the beginning do battle on fundamental questions, that is to say, on the basis of this fundamental contradiction, of the qualitative rather than quantitative needs which capitalism will never succeed in satisfying? These needs, of a potentially revolutionary urgency, exist. While the development of capitalism has made the living standard of the worker relatively more tolerable as far as individual consumption is concerned, it has made the worker's condition still more intolerable as regards the relationships of production and of work, that is to say as regards his alienation in the largest sense, the sense not only of exploitation, but also of oppression, of dehumanization. It is this intolerable alienation that needs to be brought more profoundly into consciousness, because it implies the negation of the worker not only as a consumer and as "generic man" but also as producer, as citizen, as a human being; and because it calls for the refusal of capitalism not only as a system of exploitation, but also as an authoritarian society with deeply rooted anti-democratic social relations, as a civilization with inverted priorities, as a system of waste and destruction. "To act politically," wrote Vittorio Foa, "is to link the alienation of the producer in the process of production to the alienation of the producer in society."

4. *The Factory and Society*

The possibility of embracing in one single perspective the condition of the worker in the process of production and in society, the possibility of returning dialectically from the immediate motives of discontent to the deeper reasons which are inherent in social relationships and in political and economic power—this possibility has appeared in a more or less explicit manner in the course of all the great mass actions of the recent past: the Walloon general strike from December 1959 to January 1960; the long struggle by Italian metal workers (May '62–February '63); the French miners' strike of the spring of 1963; the Neyrpic strike, etc., are some examples. Whether spontaneous or carefully prepared, all these actions involved, explicitly or implicitly, far greater things than the level of wages. And each in its own way demonstrated that a labor struggle is absorbed by the tactical response of management or of the State as soon as it limits itself to wage demands; it risks becoming bogged down in categorical and corporative struggles; and even if it is victorious in that regard, it risks reaching a settlement which amounts to strategic defeat.

There is a strategic defeat, in effect, every time that a great mass mobilization fails to raise the level of consciousness and the level of struggle; every time that it ends without having broken, even if only momentarily and unsuccessfully, the State's and the management's positions of power, either in society or at the place of work. Defeat, from the strategic point of view, is particularly painful when (as in the case of the French miners), State and management, after having succeeded in limiting the strike to the corporate level, yield on the question of wages while at the same time laying the foundations of an arbitration procedure governing the reasonableness of future demands.

Inversely, even when mass action fails to attain all its objectives, it gains a strategic victory when (as in the case of the Walloon workers, the Italian metal workers, and the Neyrpic strike) it sets up objectives beyond the realm of wages, when it carries on despite management concessions on wages, when it provokes a heightening of consciousness, and when it does not end before having raised additional demands, which, being unsatisfied, will resurge and reappear on a higher level in further actions.

In all these cases the possibility of designing a strategy which links the condition of the workers at the place of work with their condition in society, thus shifting the struggle away from the purely economic level (trade unionist level, which facilitates the adversary's maneuvers to divide the movement into industries and crafts, as well as permitting the "consensus" counteroffensive) toward the level of the class struggle—this possibility is inherent in the close connection which exists in the life of every worker between the three essential dimensions of his labor power:

1. *The work situation:* that is to say, the formation, evaluation, and utilization of labor power in the enterprise.

2. *The purpose of work:* i.e., the ends (or productions) for which labor power is used in society.

3. *The reproduction of labor power:* i.e., the life style and milieu of the worker, the manner in which he can satisfy his material, professional, and human needs.

No wage concession, no redistributive "social justice" can reconcile the worker with the conditions imposed on him by capital in these three dimensions. On the contrary, and this is one of the lessons of the Italian metal workers' strike: to the extent that the workers are younger, better educated, better paid, that their vital needs are better satisfied, that they have more leisure and less fear of permanent unemployment, to that extent they become more demanding on the qualitative, non-wage aspects of their condition.

Still, their demands, arising out of experience, must be made explicit and conscious so that their subjective force may become objective power. The necessarily general themes of political propaganda (or even of industrial struggles) cannot suffice; they cannot be taken as the point of departure but only as the end point, by linking the concrete condition of the worker in his work to his condition in society. The weakness of the programs of the Left has often been that even in victory its action on the institutional and legislative level has scarcely modified the condition of the workers in the productive cycle. Its result for the workers has been neither an even partial liberation within their work, nor the conquest of power, a power which would have to be extended or risk losing its substance, a power which could not be defended except by constant struggles for ever more advanced objectives.

Now, the question of workers' power is precisely what distinguishes a reform in a reformist spirit from a reform in a non-reformist spirit. To assert that every reform, so long as political hegemony does not belong to the working class, is of a reformist character and only results in a preservation of the system, making it more tolerable, is to argue from a fallacious schematicism insofar as workers' power is concerned. For while it is true that every reform (for example, nationalization and economic planning) is absorbed by the system and ends up by consolidating it so long as it leaves the power of the capitalist state intact, and as long as it leaves the execution and administration of the reform in the hands of the State alone, it is also true, inversely, that every conquest of *autonomous* powers by the working class, whether these powers be institutionalized *or not*, will not attenuate class antagonisms but, on the contrary, will accentuate them, will yield new opportunities for attacking the system, will make the system not more but less tolerable by sharpening the conflict between the human demands of the workers and the inert needs of capital. One must indeed be a poor Marxist to believe that in the framework of the capitalist relationships of production, the fundamental contradiction between labor and capital can be attenuated to the point of becoming acceptable when the workers' local conquest of power gives them a richer and more concrete consciousness of their power as a class.

In now taking up the subject of the three essential dimensions of labor power, we will attempt to make clear, in the following chapters, the inherent contradictions in the workers' condition, and the needs and demands to which this condition gives rise in the factory and in society:

—On the level of the work situation, the need to master the work and to master technological evolution, instead of being subjected to them (the refusal of oppression);

—On the level of the purpose of work, the need that work must make sense, that production be oriented toward purposeful ends (refusal of alienation of work and of the product). This will lead us to discuss the question of the economic and social priorities of the society to be constructed;

—On the level of the reproduction of labor power, the collective needs not only for consumer goods but also for social services and facilities, for autonomy, and for free time. We will thus be led to discuss the question of the civilization and of the man of the future.

CHAPTER TWO

The Work Situation

1. *Oppression*

Quite apart from the actual capitalist exploitation of labor power, the work situation is characterized in form and in content by the oppressive subordination of labor to capital.

At no matter what level and under whose direction, workers' training tends in fact to produce men who are mutilated, stunted in knowledge and responsibility. The dream of large industry is to absorb the worker from cradle to grave (from the layette at birth to the coffin at death, with job training, housing, and organized leisure in between), so as to narrow his horizon to that of his job. It is important, to begin with, not to give the worker (and not to permit him to acquire) skills superior to those which his specialized job requires. (This is "in order to avoid problems of adaptation," as an important French industrialist candidly explained at a recent management forum.) The worker must not be permitted to understand the overall production process, nor to understand work as an essentially creative act; for such thoughts might lead him to reflect, to take the initiative, and to make a decision, as for example the decision to go sell his labor power elsewhere.

For its repetitive tasks, whether those of clerks in the banks and insurance houses or those of solderers in electronics, industry requires passive and ignorant manpower. Recruited on leaving school (in a rural area, by preference) and trained either on the job or in the trade schools, this manpower will not acquire a trade which will give it professional autonomy and human dignity, but merely the skills required in the individual company which hires it. In this way the company exercises over its workers not only a kind of perpetual property right, but also the right to regulate qualifications, wages, hours, quotas, piecework, etc., as it sees fit.

Even for skilled workers, the production process nevertheless remains obscure. For the semi-skilled workers, the dominant contradiction is between the active, potentially creative essence of all work, and the passive condition to which they are doomed by the repetitive and pre-set tasks dictated by assembly line methods, tasks which transform them into worn-out accessories to the machine, deprived of all initiative. For the highly skilled workers, on the other hand, the dominant contradiction is between the active essence, the technical initiative required in their work, and the condition of passive performers to which the hierarchy of the enterprise nevertheless still condemns them.

With the exception of certain industries employing chiefly unskilled labor—industries which are rapidly declining in importance—the level of technical training required for the average job is rising; but along with his increasing technical responsibility, the worker gains no correspondingly greater mastery over the conditions to which he is subjected and which determine the manner of his work (nor, of course, is there a greater mastery over the product). Responsible for his work, he is not master of the conditions under which he carries it out. The company which hires him requires of him both creativity in the execution of his task and passive, disciplined submission to the orders and standards handed down by management.

On the margin of civil society, with its formal liberties, there thus persists behind the gates of factories, a despotic, authoritarian society with a military discipline and hierarchy which demands of the workers both unconditional obedience and active participation in their own oppression. And it is only normal that this militarized society should, on suitable occasions, assert itself as the true face of capitalist society. It tends to break out of the factory walls and to invade all domains of civil life, championing the principle of authority, the suppression of thought, criticism, speech, and assembly. In its social model, the ideal man is active but limited and submissive, having extensive skills but restricting their application to the technical domain only. We shall return to this in Chapter Four.

The oppression of the worker, the systematic mutilation of his person, the stunting of his professional and human faculties, the subordination of the nature and content of his working life to a technological evolution deliberately hidden from his powers of initiative, of control, and even of anticipation—the majority of wage demands are in fact a protest against these things. Wage demands are more often motivated by a revolt against the workers' condition itself than by a revolt against the rate of economic exploitation of labor power. These demands translate the desire to be paid as much as possible for the time being lost, the life being wasted, the liberty being alienated in working under such conditions; to be paid as much as possible not because the workers value wages (money and all it can buy) above everything else, but because, at the present stage of union activity, only the price of labor power may be disputed with management, but not control over the conditions and nature of work.

In short, even when highly paid, the worker has no choice but to sell his skin, and therefore he tries to sell it as dearly as possible. And inversely, no matter what price he receives for selling his liberty, that price will never be high enough to make up for the dead loss which he suffers in qualitative and human terms; even the highest pay will never restore to him control over his professional life and the liberty to determine his own condition.

The simple wage demand thus appears as a distortion and a mystification of a deeper demand; exclusive concentration on the pay envelope is an impasse into which the labor movement is headed. For the movement is going in precisely the direction management wants: it is abandoning to management the power of organizing the production process, the quantitative and qualitative content of working hours and of working conditions as they see fit, in exchange for bonuses to "compensate" for the increased mutilation of the working man. The movement thus accepts the fundamental criteria of the profit economy, namely that everything has a price, that money is the supreme value, that any and everything may be done to men provided they are paid. The movement is becoming increasingly "Americanized," as the European management wants it to be: the workers abandon all efforts to control and transform the relations of production, the organization of the productive process and capitalist control of the enterprise; they leave the company free to pursue its maximum profit and to reign unchallenged over society, receiving in exchange occasional large crumbs from capital's head table. The working class movement is allowing industry to produce a new mass of lobotomized proletarians whom eight hours of daily degradation and of work by the clock leaves with only a weary desire for escape, an escape which the merchants and manipulators of leisure time and culture will sell them on credit even in their homes, persuading them in the bargain that they are living in the best of all possible worlds.

In truth, if the working class wishes to preserve its potential as the ruling class, it must first of all attack the workers' condition on the job, because it is there, where the worker is most directly alienated as producer and citizen, that capitalist society can be most immediately challenged. Only by a conscious rejection of oppressive work conditions, by a conscious decision to submit these conditions to the control of the associated workers, by an unceasing effort to exercise autonomous self-determination over the conditions of labor, can the working class maintain or assert permanently the autonomy of its consciousness as a class, and the human emancipation of the worker as a supreme end.

The achievement of workers' autonomy within the productive process, writes Vittorio Foa,

> is the most important point of union strategy, [and] the point around which democracy in an industrial society revolves. The organization of labor tends toward an increasing dissociation of decision from execution; it makes the worker into a simple, docile instrument, without control over the process of production as a whole or over its external connections. This organization tends, in other words, to subordinate the worker rigidly to the profit-oriented decisions of the employer. Even the worker's desire for a fairer share of the national product is used against him, with his complicity, to transform him into a particular type of consumer; and the resulting mass consumption increases the profits of the system.

However well developed the political institutions may be, the law of production tends increasingly to be independent of political democracy, independent of the rights of free thought, free press, free association, etc. Experience shows that this fundamental lack of liberty in the modern work situation is a permanent menace to public liberties.

Some people think that this subordination of workers is an inevitable consequence of the modern organization of production, as inevitable in a socialist regime as in a capitalist one, that this signifies that all industrial society must be condemned, and that this subordination will perhaps not be overcome until the post-industrial society, when human labor has been replaced by machines. We do not believe in this inevitability; we believe that collective action can achieve democracy. Others think that oppression arises exclusively from private appropriation of the means of production, and that once public expropriation of capital has been achieved, the workers' liberty will be automatically assured. This also seems to us inexact: socialist power can expropriate the private capitalist and create in this way the premises of workers' liberty; but if the organization of production in the enterprise and in the total economy remains bureaucratized with a rigid system of centralized decision making, then the workers will continue to experience social production as an alien process and will find themselves in a subordination in certain ways similar to that in the capitalist countries.

The problem of industrial society, with its advanced organization of production and of labor, is the problem of the democratic organization of the worker's condition at work, the problem of workers' self-determination of their future and of their present, their work situation, the quantitative and qualitative content of their performance, and thus also self-determination of the social reproduction of their labor power. At the monopoly stage of capitalism it is no longer possible to oppose the power of the State to that of private monopolies: the masses no longer cling to illusions on this subject. At the monopoly stage of capitalism, the construction of democracy must also find forms of expression which, stemming from the workers' condition, embrace it in its entirety and thereby embrace the entire human condition.

Thus the problem of democracy in industrial society can await neither post-industrial society nor socialism. It should be faced in the present. And this is precisely what the highest level of union struggle is doing today.[1]

2. *Counter-Powers*

But what is this highest level? How can the mass struggle for the workers' victory over the oppression they suffer in their work and in their life at work be waged? In France, some good, generous souls believe they have found the answer: one must fight for the recognition of the citizen's formal liberties (freedom of assembly, speech, and publication), on the job, in short, for the legal recognition of the workers' organization within the company. This is simply posing the question backward and believing it thus solved. If the unions were the concrete expression of the workers' liberty (or of the promise of liberation), if they were capable of elaborating objectives which would mobilize the workers toward self-determination of their condition, the problems of recruitment and union militancy—the problem of establishing the union in the company—would not arise; the workers would already be struggling for control over the conditions and the organization of work, they would impose the recognition (legal or not) of their organization by force.

But the problem is precisely that French unionism has not yet succeeded in translating the struggle against oppression and for working class power into mobilizing objectives. Granted, this is difficult. That this fight was badly waged, when it was waged at all, is also evident. The struggle for the worker's emancipation in his work has remained a general and abstract idea.

In line with an old Jacobin weakness, the question has been approached from a juridical and institutional angle. At Renault, for example, in early 1963, the union added to the demand for a fourth week of paid vacation the demand for additional powers for itself. The expected happened. The management granted the fourth week for which the workers were ready to fight, but re-

[1] Vittorio Foa, "I socialisti e il sindacato" and "Considerazioni sulla vertenza dei metallurgici," *Problemi del Socialismo*, March and June, 1963.

fused the extension of union power: nobody fought for that. And they were right; the workers will fight for the union when the union says what it wants to do, concretely, with regard to the immediate and specific problems of the workers' condition, but they will not fight for it as long as it first asks for more power, in order to act later. They will fight for civil liberties in the factories (and outside) when they know what these liberties are for and what their substance will be, not before. For experience shows (notably in the United States) that when these civil liberties on the job are secured, this in itself does not increase the workers' power in the slightest. These freedoms, insofar as they are abstract and formal, can just as easily favor attempts to integrate the union into the system, to increase its bureaucratization, and to lead to union complicity with managerial paternalism (as in the USA, Sweden, and partly in West Germany).

Formal recognition of the union organization and of civil liberties on the job remains an abstract demand, incapable of mobilizing the workers as long as it is not organically linked to the demand for concrete workers' powers over the conditions of work. The former demands are not ends in themselves; the organization and its civil liberties have value only insofar as they permit the pursuit of substantial workers' powers.

And these substantial powers, as we have just indicated, consist of union control over all aspects of the work situation, in order to:

1. subordinate and adapt the exigencies of the production process to the needs of the workers;
2. narrow the sphere of management's arbitrary powers;
3. install, finally, a true workers' counter-power, capable of challenging and of positively counterbalancing the capitalist system of decision making in the company (and by extension in the society).

These three aspects, implied in the demand for workers' control over the work situation, are in fact more concrete as themes for mobilization and action than the simple wage demand which they necessarily involve. The impenetrability of the overall production process, the workers' ignorance of the economic and technical decisions which determine the conditions of their activity, force them in practice to leave the substance of their work entirely up to managerial control. In most cases, the union now negotiates nothing but the minimum price of labor power, leaving the employer free to exploit the labor force as he sees fit and to dispense premiums and bonuses over which he often has sole control and which, by definition, are not contractually negotiable.

An increase in the basic wage either has no practical effect, or may be cancelled by a number of devices, including intensification of labor (that is, the extortion of supplementary work in the same time—a speed-up), cutting various bonuses; or the introduction of new machines which make the job more complex without granting promotions and higher wages; or demoting workers on certain jobs, a demotion which may not be accompanied by a wage cut but which entails in any case a professional devaluation for the workers concerned, a halt in the development of their capacities, and the loss of autonomy in their work.

General demands for increased wages cannot, in such a situation, improve the deteriorating condition of the worker; they cannot bring about a reduction in the rate of exploitation or of profit; they cannot even measure the impact of the proposed wage increase on the rate of exploitation and of profit. But above all, in big industry, wage demands cannot adequately cover situations as diverse as those of the laborer, the semi-skilled and skilled worker, the specialist, and the technician, whose incomes vary in each case according to sex, region, city, company, and shop.

The existing great differences in working conditions and wage levels within the same industry and for the same type of work make it impossible to mobilize the working class around general and undifferentiated demands concerning the minimum and hourly rates. And in fact, the only large all-embracing workers' movements which France has known since 1954 concerned either political goals (defense of "republican liberties" or of threatened union rights) and were thus necessarily defensive protest movements which lasted only a short time, due to their lack of political outlets and of a positive program of attack; or else they were limited to the public and nationalized sectors where differences in wage levels did not exist because of the State's monopoly over employment.

This is further evidence that general and undifferentiated slogans are incapable of uniting and mobilizing a working class which itself is differentiated to an extreme; they are incapable of launching an offensive against the employers' discretionary powers over economic and technical matters, against the contradictory evolution of productivity, wages, and profits.

This is why the first task of the working class movement today is to elaborate a new strategy and new goals which will indivisibly unite wage demands, the demand for control, and the demand for self-determination by the workers of the conditions of work. The only way to unite and mobilize a differentiated working class at present is to attack the class power of the employers and of the State; and the only way to attack the class power of the employers and the State is to wrest from each employer (and from the State) a vital piece of his power of decision and control.

Concretely, the goal of this attack should not be to achieve modifications and accommodations of the workers' condition within the framework of a given management policy and a given stage in the technological development of the industry; for such a victory, besides being non-generalizable beyond the individual company, could rapidly be taken away from the workers, as rapidly as improvements in techniques and in the organization of production permit. On the contrary, the working class movement must demand permanent power to determine, by contract, all aspects of the work situation and the wage scale, so that all modifications in the productive process must be negotiated with the workers, and so that the workers can materially influence the management of the enterprise and orient it in a given direction.[2]

For example:

—The union should be able to control the training schools to ensure that they do not train robots, mutilated individuals with limited horizons and a life burdened by ignorance, but professionally autonomous workers with virtually all-sided skills, ca-

[2] For the paragraphs that follow, see notably Bruno Trentin, "Les syndicats italiens et le progrès téchnique," *Sociologie du Travail*, 2, 1962, a periodical published in Paris by the "Association pour le développement de la sociologie du travail," Éditions du Seuil, Paris.

pable of advancing in their jobs at least as fast as technological development.

—The union should be able to control the organization of work and the personnel system, to guarantee that personnel and organizational changes are made with the aim of developing the workers' faculties and professional autonomy, and not the contrary. Young workers especially should not be confined to one particularly degrading task.

—The union should thus exercise its power over the division of labor, on the company and industry level, to keep abreast of the given techniques of production and their foreseeable evolution. It should be able to impose on the employers, in each enterprise, that level and structure of employment which will result in the adoption of optimum production techniques and organization from the workers' point of view, thus guaranteeing that technological and human progress will coincide.

—The union should be able to negotiate the speed or rhythm of work, the piecework rate, the qualifications required for a job, the hours—all of which implies a continuous surveillance and negotiation of technological changes and their effects on the workers' condition, as well as the power to influence them.[3]

—Finally, the union should demand a collective output bonus, that is to say a premium which is dependent neither on individual productivity nor on profits, but on production accomplished in a fixed number of working hours. This premium, which should be added to the basic wage (and a raise in this wage should be demanded simultaneously) constitutes a first step toward workers' control over the distribution of company revenue among labor

[3] "An example of a union which does not reject technological progress, but does refuse fatalistically to submit to the forms it takes, is provided by the CGIL Federation of Textile Workers (FIOT—*Federazione Impiegati e Operai Tessili*), which, faced with the great number of new machines assigned to the workers by management, fought to include the conditions, the quantity and the quality of the work to be performed, the type of machines and their speed, the type and the quality of the product, its value, and the number of operations required of the workers in its contract negotiations." Cf. Lucio Lama, *Critica Marxista*, March 1963.

costs, investments, and amortization—that is to say, a first step toward workers' self-management.

The purpose of this collective output premium is threefold:

1. First, the object is to take out of management's hands the annual bonuses which now are distributed as presents or as "no strike payoffs" at management's pleasure and whim. These bonuses must fall within the union's power of negotiation and should be based on objective criteria.

2. The annual premium must be linked to the true level of collective productivity, that is to say, to the level of production in a fixed number of working hours. The right to negotiate this premium necessarily means that the union must have access to all information concerning the evolution of productivity in the enterprise, the real or potential evolution of profit, and, consequently, the management's policy itself.

3. On the basis of this information the union should be able to present effective opposition against any intensification of the rate of exploitation, against any enlargement in the sphere of management's power. The union will be in a position to ensure that erroneous commercial policies such as over-production or dumping will not be carried out at the expense of the workers. It will be able to adjust its demands in such a way as to limit from the beginning whatever freedom of action the employer gains by the augmentation of productivity. In the long run the union should be able to negotiate the proportions of the company budget allocated to investment, reserves, direct and indirect wages, free time, and social expenditures; and it will thus exercise a power of control and veto over the entire management policy.[4]

[4] Cf. Bruno Trentin, *op. cit.:* "Advanced industrial capitalism increasingly predetermines, in terms of a certain investment and sales program, not only the organization of labor and the hours and speed of production, but also, by deduction, even the level of wages in the company (these becoming an integral part of the production "plan"). Union action cannot therefore maintain a real autonomy unless it brings its growing weight to bear not on the *effects* of a given management policy on the workers' condition and on the economic *results* of this policy, but on the *very decisions at the moment the policy is determined.* At this moment the union has a chance

3. *The Challenge to Management*

Within the framework of this battle—whose general objectives are adaptable to each particular local situation and which embraces the most varied demands and specific problems in a single class perspective—there is quite naturally another fight, namely the battle for the recognition and autonomy of the labor organization in the enterprise. The latter is not the ultimate goal; it is rather the indispensable means which gives the workers the power to challenge and to control management policy and to determine and to impose their own policy regarding working conditions; for it is at work that the workers experience the power of capital and their conflict with society most directly. If the transformation of society and the political power of the working class are to have a meaning, then the workers must master their oppressive condition at work.

---

not only to recover damages as compensation for foreseeable modifications in the workers' condition, but also to negotiate these modifications itself, in terms of the workers' interests (of their level of employment, their need for rest, their health, their professional interests). Thus the union should recover its full autonomy of action, essentially by negotiating a part of wages, *not with regard to the results of company policy* (of which wages are always one expression), but *with regard to the decisions which precede and determine the policy itself*. . . .

"What needs to be underlined is the link which a wage policy of this nature tends to establish between the union's economic claims and efforts to assert certain forms of worker control over the policy of the enterprise. Among the possible outcomes of this policy is the union's tendency to participate as an autonomous force in predetermining the distribution of the company's revenue . . . by 'conditioning' the policy of investments and its social repercussions on the company level.

"The alternative is no longer between 'pure' unionism, which limits its action to the defense of the economic and professional interests of the workers, and a 'political' unionism which in a more or less voluntary manner orients itself toward the problems of company policy. The alternative is rather between a unionism which is integrated into a given company policy and which accepts as criteria of its action *not the real problems of the working class, but the possibilities offered by a given company policy*—and, on the other hand, a unionism which, in order to be truly autonomous and *in order to survive* realizes that its powers of negotiation must encroach on the sphere of authority, the power and the autonomy of capitalist policy."

Of course this battle will not lead to the immediate abolition of profit; it will not give *power* to the working class; it will not result in the abolition of capitalism. Victory will only lead to new battles, to the possibility of new partial victories. And at each of its stages, above all in its first phase, the battle will end with a compromise. Its path will be beset with pitfalls. The union will have to make certain agreements with management. The union will be unable to reject management's power as a whole, to challenge capitalist policy as a whole. The union will have to "dirty its hands." With each compromise, with each agreement at the end of a battle, it will endorse the employers' power with its signature.

We must not hide or minimize these facts. The dangers in the line of action which I have just outlined are real. Why then do we prefer this line to the present tactics? Let us look more closely.

Should we reject an economic policy based on profit? Should the working class take power? Should we refuse to endorse the employers' power? Of course; that goes without saying. But the workers endorse the employers' power every day, by punching in on time, by submitting to an organization of labor over which they have no power, by collecting their wages. They thereby accept the profit system; the power of the working class remains for them a dream. Does this mean, at least, that they or the union which represents them do not dirty their hands, that they remain free to reject the whole system altogether? That may be true. But their challenge and their rejection of capitalism remain on the level of general intentions and speechmaking; the challenge is abstract, its purity is sterile. The workers lack the means to turn their rhetoric into hard facts. The power of the employer and of capital remain intact. The workers lack positive accomplishments. They end up by falling into all the traps they had hoped to avoid.

For example, in order to avoid class collaboration more effectively, the union loses interest in company- and industry-wide agreements. Collective agreements are tacitly annulled or let fall into abeyance because the union does nothing to renew them when they expire. Company level agreements are not signed at the end of strikes because the union does not want to recognize the employer's power. In order not to compromise itself, the union leadership does not present a list of demands and grievances; it organizes delaying actions which express a vague discontent and diffuse protest. Then they wait for management to make offers. No negotiation with the enemy: a verbal agreement replaces a signed contract, and the union keeps its hands clean.

What does it gain from this? A clear conscience and the feeling of independence; that is to say, in practical terms—in terms of a victory over capitalist policy—nothing. And what does the employer lose? Precisely nothing: he also keeps his independence and the power to run the company as he wishes, that is, to amortize and invest according to *his* program, to install the machines which *he* wants, to impose the rhythm and organization of labor and the personnel system which seem to *him* the most advantageous, and even to pay his manpower according to the planned budget. For we must have no illusions: the safes of the modern big businesses do not contain large wads of banknotes which the workers can hope to snatch away from their greedy bosses; these safes contain only programs. And these programs have their margin of security: they are calculated in such a manner that the foreseeable wage demands will not compromise the plan of production or the plan of amortization and investment (with their predicted variations in terms of possible economic fluctuations).

The dominant tendency in large modern industry is no longer that of maximum exploitation of its workers by means such as the individual bonus and the whip. The dominant tendency (with numerous exceptions which, however, represent the past and not the future) is to "integrate the workers." The modern employer knows that the piecework system does not "pay" any more; he knows even better that in a large enterprise where fixed capital is more important than circulating capital, regularity matters more than anything else. To obtain regularity, individual output must not be stimulated too much: each increase will be followed by a decrease. Five per cent of the workers who produce double or triple the norm are less interesting than a whole shop producing one hundred per cent of the norm permanently and on the average, and this average, moreover, represents the sum of three distinct levels of effort: a third of the workers producing at eighty per cent, a third at one hundred per cent, and a final third producing at one hundred and twenty per cent of the average output, for example.

To obtain this regularity, the employer foresees the unpredictable, especially wage demands. The tactics of the "clean handed union" thus do not bother him at all. These tactics leave the employer the power which is most important to him: the power of decision and of control; the power to determine the increases to which he will be forced to consent, in order to maintain these increases within the margins which he has fixed, and to shield these margins from all effective challenge.

Thus the union falls prey to "integration" even in the demands which it advances and the concessions which it obtains. Foreseen by management's program, these demands are integrated from the beginning into the budget and encroach very little on management's policy. Nor does the union succeed in effectively challenging a planned layoff by protest movements: the cost of protest strikes is foreseen in the company budget, and the layoffs will take place as planned after the "challenge" is over. In this way union action remains without a grip on the employer's decisions and on the details of his policy, precisely because union action rejects them totally; this rejection is itself one of the elements in management's policy. And this policy remains sovereign in practice. The employer keeps the initiative: it is he who constantly confronts the union with new situations of an economic, structural, technical, or organizational order, situations which affect the professional status, the careers, the lives of the workers, situations which force them to move in the direction intended by the employer's strategy. The union has no choice but to say "yes" or "no," [5] and its "no"

[5] Sometimes the union cannot even say "no" to management offers which tie its hands, destroy its autonomy, integrate it, and buy labor peace in exchange for some material advantages.

This inability to say "no" to the worst management offers is illustrated by the agreement signed with the "Plastiques de Roubaix" company in January 1964 by the CGT, the CFTC, the General Confederation of Labor, Working Force (CGT-FO—*Confédération Générale du Travail*, "*Force* has no consequence, results in no visible progress in the succession of battles which the workers carry out. The same type of battle is always repeated, and the workers always return to the point of departure.

In this way the challenge remains abstract, does not become concrete, and does not progress. There is no meaningful link between its goals of reduction and suppression of exploitation, negotiation of all elements of wages, guarantee of employment and career, elevation of living standard according to needs, abolition of the dictatorship of profit, and its daily actions. The goals stand on one side and the actions on the other, and there is no progress from one to the other.

Ouvrière"), and the General Confederation of Permanent Employees (CGC —*Confédération Générale des Cadres*). The principal points of the agreement are:

—A productivity (not output) bonus: the benefits of productivity are distributed in equal parts among workers and management, the latter remaining master of the method of distribution (wage increase or reduction in hours);

—Profit-sharing: twenty per cent of the net profits are distributed to the employees. But management remains master of the rate of amortization and investment (and therefore of the amount of net profit). Management policy is thus entirely screened from the union (a defect which the output bonus, as we have defined it, would have avoided).

—Guaranteed monthly wages, but overtime may be demanded in exchange for working hours that have been lost due to temporary layoffs and their partial compensation.

—"Each employee, conscious that his interest is to have a smooth-running enterprise, guarantees that he will fulfill his assigned task in the prescribed conditions." Thus, no negotiation of the conditions and the organization of work, but subordination of labor to the logic of profit.

—Anti-strike clauses providing for a four-day prior notice by the union of intent to strike, followed by a labor-management conference, followed, in case the spokesmen reach no agreement, by an additional four days' notice.

—Furthermore, grievances concerning work load must be handled by "consultation" with "labor experts" under conditions "to be determined for each case separately." The union representatives are thus called on to guarantee that the workers will not eventually challenge the working conditions which management has fixed "in association" with them.

The implicit recognition of the union organization is under these conditions equivalent to a complete loss of union autonomy.

If, on the other hand, the union seizes control of the elements on the basis of which management policy is worked out, if it anticipates the employer's decisions, if at each step it presents its own alternative solution, and if it fights on that basis, then it will challenge capitalist policy more effectively than a hundred fiery speeches. The union will be in a position to exercise control over technical, productive, and professional developments, to push them in the optimum social, economic, and human direction. This means, for example, that instead of fighting *against* layoffs and reorganization plans, the union should fight *for* a plan of reorganization, reclassification, and re-employment, a plan whose every aspect is under permanent union control. Instead of fighting against new machines and the new organization of labor which these impose, it should fight over the type of machines, the process of their installation, the future organization of labor, the future job classifications, before the reorganization takes place. Instead of fighting against the intensification of exploitation, the union should fight to gain control over the program of amortization and investment to assure that the workers benefit from it.

Does the union, by acting in this way, accept the capitalist system? In a sense, it does, without a doubt; but I have already said that it also accepts the system by pretending to reject it and by enduring it. But the important thing is not to have to endure it: it must be accepted only in order to change it, to modify its bases, to counter it point by point and at each step, in order to force it to go where the workers want it to go; in short, in order to bring capitalism to a crisis and to force it to retreat to a different battlefield. And with each partial victory, with each reconversion, merger, reorganization, investment, or layoff prevented or imposed by the union, the workers' power is strengthened, the workers' level of consciousness rises; the freedom of the employers—capitalism's sphere of sovereignty—is diminished, and the essential weakness of the system is displayed: the contradiction between the logic of profit and the needs and exigencies of men.

Is this class collaboration? Unquestionably that would be the case if the union accepted the responsibilities of "cooperation" with management, if the union lost sight of its goal, which is not a little more prosperity at any price, but the emancipation of the workers and the achievement of their right to determine their own condition; it would be class collaboration if the union agreed to participate in the elaboration of policy decisions and guaranteed their execution. But precisely this participation, advocated by the "*concertistes*,"[6] must be firmly rejected. It is not a question of elaborating a neo-paternalistic company policy with management; it is a matter of opposing a union policy to that of management, of struggling for a company-, industry- and region-wide plan, a well-elaborated and coherent plan, one which demonstrates concretely the opposition between the desirable and the possible, on the one hand, and a profit-oriented reality on the other hand.

Clearly, the battle must be concluded with a settlement, a compromise. The only ones to be shocked by this would be the left wing extremists, with whom Lenin already clashed, pointing out that there are good compromises and bad compromises. Under the circumstances, compromise would be bad if the union renounced its plan and its perspectives, in order to settle for an intermediate solution. But why should it renounce its plan? The settlement which concludes the battle simply signifies that all of the plan's objectives could not be obtained: the union has reached a compromise on the basis of the employer's adoption of a substantial part of its plan; and the union exercises its control over this plan. Thus the battle ends with a partial victory, won by force, and with a "moral" victory which, in this case, is complete. For in the course of the struggle, the workers' level of consciousness has risen; they know perfectly well that all their demands are not satisfied, and they are ready for new battles. They have experienced their power; the measures which they have imposed on management go in the direction of their ultimate demands (even though they did not obtain complete satisfaction). By compromising they do not renounce their goal; on the contrary, they move closer to it. By reaching a settlement the union does not alienate its autonomy (no more than when it accepts an eight

[6] "*Concertistes*" are advocates of closer cooperation between labor and management. [Translators' note.]

per cent raise although it had asked for twelve per cent); it does not endorse management's plan; on the contrary, it forces management to guarantee (with union control) the execution of the essentials of the union plan.

Such is the strategy which begins to establish the power of the union to negotiate all aspects of the work situation, to diminish thereby the autonomy of the employer and, by extension, the class power of management and the State. This is not an institutional union power; it is rather a positive and antagonistic power of challenge which leaves union autonomy intact. This power, once it is achieved after necessarily long and hard struggles,[7] will establish a permanent and continuous challenge to management decisions; it will permit the union to anticipate these decisions, to influence them before they are made; it will place the workers in an offensive, not a defensive position; it will elevate their level of consciousness and competence; it will deepen their knowledge of the productive process; it will force them to specify their goals, scaled according to a strategic and programmatic vision, goals which they intend to oppose to the capitalist plan on the company, industry and regional levels, and on the level even of the national economy; it will give rise to partial and local demands (which is today not the case) within the framework of an overall and coherent perspective of response ("alternative") to monopoly capitalism, a perspective which will reciprocally influence and clarify the local demands; and in this way it will stimulate a continually resurging struggle with more and more advanced goals, at a higher and higher level.

Thus, the demand for workers' power in the enterprise does not necessarily signify the development of particularism or of company "patriotism." [8] On the contrary, this demand will have a militant and mobilizing substance, a meaning and a chance of

[7] The struggle of one million Italian metal workers for these goals lasted nine months, including the equivalent of 42 days of strike. During five of these nine months, the goal was to achieve measures of workers' control over management, a goal which the management tried to dissociate from the *general* wage demands which it was willing to meet.

[8] This particularism at present develops precisely because a perspective which tightly links local demands to class action is lacking.

success, insofar—but insofar only—as it is conceived as a local adaptation of an overall response to the model of capitalist development. This demand requires such an overall vision to be effective on the political level (on the level of the big decisions regarding national development and economic policy), just as political action requires the support of mobilized and militant masses; it requires this vision not only in order to make progress, but also and above all in order to establish itself as a popular counterpower capable of overcoming the obstructive power of the private and public centers of decision making in a decentralized and nonbureaucratic manner.

Thus, the demand for and the exercise of workers' power, of self-determination and control, quite naturally lead to a challenge of the priorities and purposes of the capitalist model.

CHAPTER THREE

The Purpose of Work

THE QUESTION OF THE DESTINATION assigned to labor power by capitalism has already constantly arisen, in however implicit a manner, in discussing the content of the work situation. And the theme that was outlined in this regard was that of the meaning of work, or, more explicitly, that of its aims. The formal contradiction between the active, potentially creative essence of work, and the passive status of merchandise conferred on it by the capitalist in the process of arbitrarily and despotically disposing of the professional life of the worker through the relationships, conditions, and organization of labor—this formal contradiction, which is experienced as oppression, goes hand in hand with a substantial contradiction: the contradiction between the intrinsic purpose of work from the viewpoint of the worker (that is, by the application of his labor power to materials to produce wealth which has a human value and to produce man as the universal producer in the same process) and its extrinsic purpose from the viewpoint of capital, that is, to produce surplus value in the process of producing something, no matter what (the use value of the product being secondary to its profitability) and, at the same time, to produce producers who submit to the exploitation of their labor power as if the latter were a strange and hostile quantity; that is to say, to produce alienated men. In brief, for the worker, work has no meaning except as the production of a human world; for capital, work has no meaning except as the production of profits, regardless of the human utility of the products by means of which profit is realized.

The worker's condition is therefore inacceptable not only by virtue of the direct oppression of labor in productive life, but also and equally because of the negation of the meaning of productive life, due to the purpose which capitalist exploitation assigns to work: because of alienation. Every worker more or less consciously experiences this alienation as the contradiction between his pride in and love for a piece of work well done on the one hand, and on the other hand, the shame, anger, or despair at having to accomplish this work for purposes (capitalist accumulation) and for products which often are not worth the trouble and which correspond neither to real or priority needs, nor to the interests of the collectivity.

1. *Concrete Alternatives*

The struggle against exploitation does not take on its full meaning until it becomes a conscious struggle against the social consequences of exploitation, that is to say, a struggle against the false priorities, the waste and deprivation that monopoly capitalism in its mature phase imposes on society as the so-called model of "affluent consumption." To struggle against the exploitation of labor is necessarily to struggle also against the purposes for which labor is exploited.

The separation of these two aspects is less possible than ever if the labor movement wants to conserve its autonomy. In effect, a labor organization which, on the pretext that politics is none of its business, tries to channel the workers' actions solely into demands for higher consumption, and, implicitly, into the struggle against exploitation, would logically be led to look with favor—or at least without principled hostility—on proposals made by the capitalist state to integrate labor organizations into the system, to discuss with them an eventual ceiling on the profit rate, eventually to link the level of wages to the expansion of the national income, without challenging either the overall cost of capitalist accumulation, or the driving role of profit, either the political-economic power of the monopolies or the orientations and priorities forced upon all economic activity by the urge to maximize profits.

In addition, to struggle against exploitation and in favor of demands for greater consumption, but without challenging the purposes of exploitation (i.e., accumulation) and the model and the hierarchy of consumption in advanced capitalist society, is to place the working class in a subordinate position with regard to the fundamental decisions, the values, the ideology of this society, and to reinforce the latter even with the minor successes achieved by the unions. In effect, these successes—increase in wages, in vacation time, in the amount of individual consumption—will rapidly be made into a paying proposition by those (government and monopolies) who granted them; they rapidly become a source of additional profits (with or without a rise in prices) for the consumer goods industry. So long as they remain only quantitative and not also qualitative, economic struggles remain unable to affect the system profoundly, and contribute very little to forging and raising class consciousness.[1]

Before indicating how questions of purpose (regarding the structure and orientation of consumption and production) become concretely felt by the worker, and how such questions can supply the content for qualitative demands, we will show the insufficiency of quantitative struggles by means of a few examples. Consider, for instance, the pressure exercised by American labor organizations (in concert with management, by the way) to keep in operation certain armaments industries (aviation, manufacture of ammunition and tanks) which have become obsolete and are scheduled to shut down, and this with a great show of patriotic and militarist arguments. This narrow conception of collective defense of work and employment, however, goes hand in hand with an individual, powerless revolt by the workers against the absurdity of their work. On the assembly lines of the American automobile industry, this revolt extends as far as clandestine acts of sabotage against a product (the automobile body) which appears to the worker as the detestable materialization of the social uselessness and individual absurdity of his toil.[2] Along the same lines is the less extreme and more complex example of miners fighting with admirable perseverance against the closing of the mines where they are exploited under inferior human and economic

[1] Cf. Foa: "What counts is not the overall comparison between the level of consumption and the level of investments, but the distribution and internal composition of consumption and investment." "Politica salariale e sviluppo economico," in *Economia e Sindacato*, theoretical publication of the CGIL, 1961–1963, September 1961.

[2] Cf. Harvey Swados, "The Myth of the Happy Worker," *The Nation*, August 17, 1957, pp. 117, 119.

conditions—but who, individually, have no difficulty in recognizing that even if the coal they produced were not so bad and so expensive, their job, under the prevailing conditions, would still be abominable.

Finally, it is clear from these examples of purely defensive actions that working class action does not spontaneously result in—and even that it stops short and dies away if it does not have—a perspective on the political level which ties the immediate grievances together in a strategic overall vision of class relationships, thus linking immediate objectives to longer range, broader objectives, namely the transformation of society. Precisely these cases of partial or complete shutdown, of geographical transfer, of reconversion, and of newly installed plants—cases which will become more and more frequent due to the influence of technological evolution and of monopolistic competition in the Common Market—impose on the working class the necessity to fight in the name of an "alternative" to the policies and priorities of the monopolies, to fight with a greater emphasis on demands for qualitatively different solutions. Failing that, in such a case the labor struggle can hardly go beyond the level of defensive, rear guard, nearly desperate battles.

Shutdowns, reconversions, and new installations (or the absence of new industries) also offer the labor movement an excellent opportunity to assert its leading role in society by pointing to the often dramatic difficulties into which the decisions of monopoly capital plunge the workers and the whole population of the affected area. Outlining the remedy for these difficulties, the optimum solution, from the human viewpoint as well as from the point of view of economic equilibrium and of regional development, the movement will prove easily that decisions are needed which run counter to the logic of capitalism; that the optimum solution demands "structural reforms" which modify the relationship of forces, the redistribution of functions and powers, new centers of democratic decision making—aims which prefigure a socialist transformation of society and move toward it.

It is again the Italian labor movement, in its syndicalist and political elements, which offers clear examples of this kind of qualitative demand, which propose an alternative line to the policy of monopolist development. Among the cases which have become famous is that of a big mechanical construction enterprise at Reggio Emilia, condemned to be shut down as part of the Marshall Plan, whose entire personnel (workers and staff) occupied the plant, threw out the management, and, making use of abandoned projects, organized the production of agricultural tractors on its own initiative. It took several months before the first tractors came off the assembly lines. During this entire time, the company was able to keep going thanks to the funds raised among the peasant and urban population of the region. A rough-hewn Commune, this venture was finally refinanced by the State, under the pressure of the working class parties. For a time it continued to build tractors, and was then reconverted and expanded. It still exists.

Another example is that of the proposed coastal steel complexes. Their construction by the state was long demanded locally and regionally by the CGIL, with strikes and mass demonstrations. These actions, which mobilized the entire population, were an essential factor in the economic development of declining or underdeveloped regions. Supported on the national level by the workers' parties, they succeeded in creating a public body set up to finance certain of these complexes, which the state had at first decreed uneconomical. The struggle for the coastal steel works was based on a very carefully elaborated plan, but the projects finally approved by the state have remained less advanced than this plan. None of these battles ended with a total victory for the labor movement. But alone the fact of having waged this struggle, with partial successes which were often considerable, has made it possible to carry class conflict to a higher and more dramatic level. This struggle has made it possible to advance and to demonstrate the feasibility of an alternative to the line of monopolist expansion; it has made the working masses conscious, during these battles, of their power as a class, of the insufficiency and vulnerability of the capitalist system, and of the necessity to overcome it, a natural perspective arising out of the very heart of everyday struggles.

The fight for structural reforms (permanent acquisitions during the advance toward socialist democracy) and for intermediate objectives arising out of the direct prolongation of immediate struggles (those which make explicit the possibility, the advantages, and the necessity of an alternative line), is thus essential to the development of actions which will bore from within and make clear the internal contradictions of the capitalist process in order to bring it to the crisis point. Though waged from within the capitalist process, the fight for structural reforms creates possibilities which point beyond capitalism and which therefore render the status quo all the more intolerable, its contradictions and shortcomings more evident. It goes without saying that this struggle cannot be confined to the level of Parliament and its parties, as if it were only a political and ideological battle. For not only does Parliament tend to be deprived of real powers and the labor representation diminished by gerrymandering and other maneuvers; but also, political and ideological struggles are effective only if their objectives, instead of appearing as mirages of the more or less distant future, are geared to potential or ongoing mass actions whose concrete objectives the political battles amplify.[3]

In other words, an alternative line must appear as a concrete and positive possibility, attainable through the pressure of the masses on all levels:

—On the shop level, through the conquest by the workers of power over the organization and condition of work;

—On the company level, by the conquest of a workers' coun-

[3] The fight against the *force de frappe* (French nuclear striking force), for example, will remain mere agitation and abstract propaganda so long as the labor movement has not worked out, factory by factory, industry by industry, and on the level of the national planning, a program of reconversion and reorientation of the armament industries.

Lacking such a program, not only will the workers rightly fear for their jobs in case of a Leftist victory, but also the Left, once in power, will be either incapable of ending the *force de frappe* program in order not to throw thousands of workers onto the street, or it will be torn between the political desire to abandon the program and the pressure from the unions at the factory level for whom the existing program has come to mean the defense of their employment.

ter-power concerning the rate of profits, the volume and orientation of investments, technical level and evolution;

—On the industry and sector level, by the fight against overinvestment, fraught with future crises; and the fight against the shortcomings of capitalist initiative as regards the development of socially necessary production; both fights having to be linked to a program of industrial reorientation and/or reconversion;[4]

—On the level of the city, by the struggle against the monopolies' stranglehold over the entire life of the town (cultural, social, economic), over public transports, real estate and housing, city administration,[5] the organization of leisure, etc.;

—On the provincial level, by the struggle for new industries which are necessary to the survival and the equilibrium of the region, the absorption of open or hidden unemployment, the creation of jobs for the workers whose industries undergo crises or are about to disappear. This fight should mobilize farmers as well as workers, should be based on an alternate program of regional development, directed by the unions and the labor parties jointly, and should aim at the establishment of regional centers of decision making which are independent both of monopoly capital and of the centralizing tendencies of the state;

—On the level of the national Plan,[6] that is to say on the level

[4] On these two points, see for example the interesting attempt by Gilbert Declerq concerning the construction in the Loire-Atlantique of a public steel and machine-tool industry, in order to resolve the problem created by the crisis in the shipyards and to break the employment monopoly of the latter.

[5] On this subject, see especially Pierre Belleville, *Une Nouvelle Classe Ouvrière* (Coll. Les Temps Modernes), Julliard 1963, above all the chapters about the Lorraine and the North.

[6] *Le Plan*, i.e., government economic planning, was started in 1946 with the establishment of the Planning Commission (*Commissariat du Plan*) by de Gaulle's Provisional Government. The officially stated aim was to work out a complete program for modernizing and reequipping the economy of France and its overseas territories, so as to overcome the effects of the war and of many years of economic stagnation prior to the war. The recommendations of the Commission had, and still have, no mandatory power, but the government backs them up with fiscal measures and other controls. Four Plans have been presented so far, essentially providing direction for public

of society, finally, by the elaboration of an alternative Plan which modifies the orientation given to the economy by State and monopoly capitalism, which reestablishes real priorities that conform to social needs, and which challenges the purposes of private accumulation and of the "consumers' society" by developing the human resources (education, research, health, public installations, city planning) and the material resources of the nation.

2. *Squalor Within Affluence*

On this subject, one can never emphasize sufficiently the fact that social, cultural, and regional underdevelopment on the one hand and the rapid development of "affluent" consumer goods industries on the other are two sides of the same reality. If collective facilities, social and public services (urban public transport, among other things), education, regional, and rural development are generally in a state of scandalous deficiency, while at the same time the oligopolies which produce articles for individual consumption enjoy a spectacular prosperity, the reason is not that the former are public and the latter private. On the contrary, it is because State-monopoly capitalism secures for the latter the driving role in economic development; because private accumulation diverts the greatest part of surplus value toward investments which yield a short-term profit; and because the portion of surplus value which can be utilized for social investment, for the satisfaction of priority necessities, therefore becomes insufficient.

In addition, the capitalist State subordinates its own investments, already insufficient in volume, to the interests of the monopolies: by pre-financing their expansion, by creating the infrastructure for them, by helping the monopolies (through its price, financial, fiscal, and military policies) to find a market for their anarchical productions. Always two steps behind, the State tries its best to finance out of public funds the social cost of private accumulation (urban congestion, transportation, professional edu-

---

and private investment. One of the main goals is to expand production in order to make the French economy competitive in the Common Market economy. [Publisher's note.]

cation, infrastructure, public health, etc.) and, unable to catch up, cuts down those public investments (cultural, social, and industrial) which because they are relatively autonomous would be in a position to counteract the monopolist line of development. (For a further discussion, see Part Two.)

The solution of the structural, social, and cultural problems of the society cannot therefore be found by the creation of new public bodies, but only by subjecting the principal existing centers of decision making and of accumulation to public control, for the purpose of socializing the investment and accumulation functions themselves. And, when this same State demands of the workers a contractual wage discipline, in the name of the famous consumption-investment equilibrium, the answer to be given is clear:

1. Under present conditions there exists no guarantee whatsoever that decreased consumption will result in increased investment. On the contrary, wage discipline can have the effect of welding business into a united front, of guaranteeing superprofits including those drawn from increased productivity for the monopolies, and of discouraging scientific and technological research.

2. Even assuming that accumulated profits are actually invested, nothing guarantees that they will be invested in a rational and socially useful manner in the regions, industries, and services where they are socially most needed.

3. It is possible to increase at the same time, for a period, both the level of consumption (individual and collective) of the working masses and the level of socially useful investments, on condition that the internal, qualitative structure of consumption and investment be modified, that sumptuary consumption and investment be restricted, that speculative and parasitical revenues be suppressed (especially in the commercial and real estate sectors), and that waste in all its forms be reduced by the socialization of the investment function.

So long as the State has not become the master of the real driving forces of the economy, so long as the organized working class cannot orient the development of the economy toward the satisfaction of priority needs, so long as by subordinating its action to that of the monopolies—by granting the latter profits without risks—the State permits waste of social products for sumptuary or simply uneconomic purposes, just so long does the labor movement have the right, and even the duty, of refusing categorically all "wage discipline" and all economic consensus making measures whose only effect would be to perpetuate the exploitation of labor power, the appropriation and misuse of surplus value by the monopolies.

The influence of the latter is felt, in effect, more or less openly in all spheres of civil life. And this is true not only because within certain limits the monopolist sector controls the prices of the products it sells as well as of the products and services it buys, and appropriates to itself an important part of the surplus value of other sectors (agriculture and industrial sub-contractors notably, as well as of the energy producing, mining, and transport sectors); but also because of the fact that the monopolist sector is in a position to impose a model of production and of consumption, and to orient the tastes of the "consumers" toward products which permit the highest profit rate, by the forced sale of services and goods; we will return to this subject in Chapter Four. The results are the disparities and distortions common to all the State-monopoly capitalist economies: "public squalor within private affluence," to use Galbraith's phrase: megalopolis with gigantically expensive infrastructures and operations, and decline (going as far as the creation of wastelands) in so-called eccentric regions; slums with television and/or means of individual transport; illiteracy (real or figurative) and transistor radios; rural underdevelopment and superhighways; cities with neither hygiene, fresh air, nor sunlight, but with commercial cathedrals, etc.

The de facto dictatorship of the monopolies over all domains of economic and cultural activity is not, of course, exercised in a direct manner: it passes through a certain number of intermediate steps, it asserts itself essentially through the priorities it controls, by the subordination and conditioning of the range of human needs according to the inert exigencies of capital. Bourgeois ideologists sometimes attempt to deny this relationship of subordination by pointing to the sphere of autonomy (often real, incidentally) enjoyed by the State or by corporate bodies like universities. And it is true that to speak of a dictatorship of the monopolies over the State and over education, for example, is to oversimplify matters. The State plays the role of enlightened mediator between the direct interests of the monopolies and those of society; and this mediating role can include steps which seem to go contrary to the immediate interests of monopoly capital. In the short run, it is in the constant interest of monopoly capital to limit to a strict minimum all the activities of the public sector (education, health, hygiene, city planning, cultural and sports facilities, etc.) since the latter divert resources which have been deducted from individual income and buying power toward social uses from which no accumulation or profit can be realized. State-financed social consumption not only deflates or threatens to deflate the volume of surplus value, it also prevents a portion of individual buying power from flowing into the cash registers of private companies. It virtually creates a circuit of money not subject to the laws of the market and of capitalist profitability, a sector which is virtually antagonistic to the profit economy. (We shall return to this subject. See also, in Part Two, "The Alternative.")

A permanent antagonism, therefore, opposes private capital to the State, even the capitalist State, as public entrepreneur active in unproductive, unprofitable sectors of general interest. But precisely what distinguishes neo-capitalism from traditional capitalism is that the former recognizes the necessity of the mediating role of the State; its efforts no longer aim at restraining public initiative, but at orienting it and even developing it for the benefit of monopoly accumulation. It is in the long-term interest of monopoly capital to insure that occasional redistributions of income render the capitalist system socially tolerable that health and public hygiene slow the exhaustion of labor power, that public education cover future needs for trained manpower, that public city transportation, financed by the entire population, deliver manpower to the factories in good condition, that nationalization of energy sources and raw materials place onto the shoulders of the entire population the burden of supplying industrial needs at low cost. The expansion of public activity, in short, is welcome so long as it limits itself to publicly pre-financing the basis of monopoly expansion and accumulation; so long, that is, as it remains in a subordinate position to private capital and abandons to the latter the responsibility of determining the dominant orientations of the economy.

But that means precisely that the satisfaction of social and cultural needs is never considered as an end in itself, but only in a utilitarian manner; that the full development of human faculties (through education, research, information, and culture) including urban and rural development, is not pursued as a priority. These activities are developed only to the degree that they complement private initiative, or at least do not oppose its interests; or so long as they do not lead individuals to challenge the system. True enough, the University may be free, opposition and dissent may be voiced. Dissenters—mainly if they are celebrated writers or artists—are an essential ornament of neo-capitalist society. But an ornament only. Information is directed by the State or (in practice) by commercial interests; cultural facilities belong to the corporations or to the Church; publishing submits to the laws of the market and to pre- or self-censorship.

Economic, cultural, and social development are not oriented toward the development of human beings and the satisfaction of their social needs as a priority. but *first* toward the creation of those articles which can be sold with the maximum profit, regardless of their utility or lack of utility. Creative activity is limited by the criteria of financial profitability or of social stability,[7] while millions of hours of work are wasted in the framework of monopoly competition in order to incorporate modifications in consumer products, modifications which are often marginal but always costly,[8] and which aim at increasing neither the use value nor the esthetic value of the product.

[7] To a large extent, only the fear of being surpassed by the USSR has precipitated in the advanced capitalist countries the thrust toward automation, a development laden with explosive social problems for capitalism.

[8] The American automobile industry spends annually $500 million for marginal modifications of its models, while at the same time limiting their

The social repercussions of the process of production on all aspects of life—work condition, leisure, education, entertainment and mass consumption, city planning—are not absorbed by any social project tending to humanize the social process, to give it meaning, to further social aims. The social processes, instead of being dominated and governed by human society, dominate *it;* they appear as "accidental" social results of private decisions and they proliferate anarchically: dormitory-cities, urban congestion, internal migrations, various kinds of misery and luxury. Instead of putting production at the service of society, society is put at the service of capitalist production: the latter endeavors with all its ingenuity to offer to individuals ever-new means of evading this intolerable social reality; and the implementation on a grand scale of these individual means of escape (automobiles, private houses, camping, passive leisure) thereby recreates a new anarchic social process, new miseries, inverted priorities, and new alienation.

Mature capitalist society, therefore, remains profoundly barbaric as a *society*, to the degree that it aims at no civilization of social existence and of social relationships, no culture of social individuals, but only a civilization of individual consumption. Simultaneously, the homogeneity and the stereotypes of individual consumption created by the oligopolies produce this particular social individual whose social nature appears to him as accidental and alien: the individual in a mass society.

One must not take this to mean—as sentimentalists of the age of artisans imply—that mass production itself induces the "massification" of social individuals. The latter is in no sense an inevitable consequence of assembly line production methods. It is, rather, the consequence of production which is social in its form but not in its ends. It is one thing to produce mass quantities of low priced agricultural equipment, mechanical pencils for the schools, work clothes, and lunch boxes—products which are designed to satisfy social needs as such, and which a social production is called upon to supply. It is another thing to work not for society but for a

life, through "planned obsolescence" and without any saving of money, to about 40,000 miles. See Vance Packard's *The Waste Makers* (New York: McKay, 1960).

private company, producing objects which will satisfy no social need but will be offered to individual buyers as symbols of their liberation from social pressures.

For that is, in the last analysis, the mystique on which so-called affluent capitalism is based: production, which is social in form, scope, and consequence, never appears as such; it denies the social character of "demand," of work, and of needs which individuals have in common, which social production enriches and develops. What capitalism offers is consumer goods which are artificially and radically cut off from work and from the conditions of production which created them. And it does this for a reason: as a consumer, the individual is encouraged to escape his condition as a social producer, to reconstitute himself as a *private* microcosm which he can enjoy and over which he can reign as solitary sovereign.

The ideology implied by the model of "affluent" consumption is less that of comfort than that of the monad cooped up in its lonely, self-sufficient universe: the home with "all modern facilities" (a closed universe independent of external services) where one can look on the world as an outsider (thanks to television), which one leaves at the wheel of a private automobile to go enjoy "nature without people"—while venting anger against "the State" which does not build enough highways to make this escape easier; anger against the State, but not against the profit economy which makes this escape almost a necessity. The negation of the social origin and character of human needs, the negation of the necessarily social mode of their satisfaction, and the affirmation of the possibility of individual liberation through the acquisition of means of escape (whose social production is carefully masked) are the fundamental mystifications of the so-called affluent civilization.

The underlying reason for the "massification" of individuals is to be found in this refusal to take care of the social reality of individual life, a reality which is pushed back into the outer shadows, into the realm of the "accidental." This massification is the powerless and anarchic solitude of separated individuals, who suffer their social nature as if it were an external statistical reality, and who are manipulated in their individual behavior by the specialists of "hidden persuasion."

3. *Conditioned Consumers*

Even if they do not always go to the root of the problem, some very intelligent things have been said by the Catholic extreme left on the subject of the alienation of the individual in a mass society, the individual as passive consumer.[9] I will briefly summarize these writings.

The existence of unsatisfied primary needs until now furnished the capitalist mode of production with a natural base and a human purpose, at least in appearance and objectively. The bulk of demand in fact required products necessary for the reproduction of life; and whatever its peculiar internal logic may have been, capitalist production was objectively based on primary needs which maintained their autonomy. This natural base, furnished to the system by a preexisting demand, could, to a certain degree, make credible the claim that the economy was in the service of consumption and had its human rationality as a science which practiced the utilization of scarce resources with a view to their increase.[10] In fact, the natural basis of demand masked the intrinsic ends of capitalist production, i.e., the accumulation of surplus—the specific exigency and end-in-itself of the system. But what was concealed while the necessary means of life were lacking, appears clearly when these primary needs have for the most part been satisfied, when in any case they no longer constitute an ex-

[9] See especially Claudio Napoleone and Franco Rodano, *Rivista trimestrale*, No. 1–4 (Via Lazio 9, Rome); also Lucio Magri, *Les Temps Modernes*, September–October 1962, pp. 608–610.

[10] Following Piero Sraffa (whose latest work is *Production of Commodities by Means of Commodities: Prelude to a Critique of Economic Theory*, Cambridge University Press, 1960), Claudio Napoleone was able to show that economic theory cannot coherently account for the capitalist system unless it treats wages as a dependent, predetermined, and fixed quantity, and consumption as a subordinate factor in relation to accumulation (see *Rivista trimestrale*, No. 1). Demonstrations along the same line could be made with regard to the neo-colonialist efforts to induce economic development according to capitalist principles, especially in Latin America.

panding demand, and when the expansion of production therefore loses its vitally necessary character and its natural basis.

Under these new conditions, individuals freed from natural necessity in theory arrive at the possibility of choosing the nature of the wealth to be produced, the possibility of producing for consciously creative human ends and no longer for natural human ends; the possibility of submitting the mode and the apparatus of production, as well as production itself, to the requirement of producing "human men"; and finally, the possibility of concentrating essentially on creativity in production as well as in consumption, whereas creativity has been so far a necessarily subordinate element.

Now—for reasons which we will indicate later—monopoly capitalism has succeeded in preventing this subordination of production to creative activity, in stifling all creative activity, and in perpetuating, as in the period of general scarcity, the subordination of consumption to the exigencies of the production process. As Marx had foreseen, monopoly capitalism found itself faced with the problem of shaping subjects for the objects to be marketed; not of adjusting supply to demand, but demand to supply.

It has solved this problem by conditioning individuals to suit the most profitable production—not only in their individual needs but equally in their perception of the world (their conception of the State, society, civilization, coexistence with other societies and civilizations, etc.). In order to harness society for purposes of private accumulation, on the level of individual consumption as well as of public consumption (government spending), it has made every effort to extend its dictatorship to all aspects and every sphere of private life, to become the master of individuals in their work, their leisure, their home, in the schools, in the information available to them, in the way in which they reproduce their labor power, in their relationships with other human beings. By the extension of its dictatorship to culture, to private life, to local and national institutions, monopoly capitalism has finally appeared in its true light: as a system which requires production for the sake of production, i.e., accumulation for the sake of accumulation, a system which requires a society of compulsory consumption. And also, to be sure, a system which requires a type of individual susceptible to the pressures designed to make him a passive consumer: mass individuals on whom the system can impose purposes, desires, and wishes by which to manipulate them.

But if we limit our analysis to these aspects of "affluent capitalism" we remain on the surface only of the phenomenon. Its root is in the capitalist relationships of production. In truth, the "alienated consumer" is an "individual who reflects in his need for consumption his alienation as an agent of production."[11] The alienated consumer is one and the same as the manual, intellectual, or white collar worker who is cut off from his fellow workers made passive by the military discipline of the factory, cut off from his product, ordered to sell his time, to execute with docility a pre-fabricated task, without worrying about the purposes of his work. The passive and "massified" consumer required by capitalist production in order to subordinate consumption is not created by capitalism altogether by means of advertising, fashion, and "human relations," as is often asserted; on the contrary, capitalism *already* creates him within the relationships of production and the work situation by cutting off the producer from his product; and, what is more, by cutting the worker off from his work, by turning this work against him as a certain pre-determined and alien quantity of time and trouble which awaits the worker at his job and requires his active passivity.

It is because the worker is not "at home" in "his" work, because this work, negated as a creative activity, is a calamity, a pure *means* of satisfying needs, that the individual's active and creative needs are amputated, and he no longer finds his sphere of sovereignty except in non-work, that is to say in the satisfaction of passive needs, in consumption, and in domestic life.[12]

[11] Bruno Trentin, *Tendenze del Capitalismo italiano*, I (conclusions), Editori Riuniti, Rome, 1962.

[12] I have been paraphrasing Marx: "What constitutes the alienation of labor? First, that the work is *external* to the worker, that it is not part of his nature; and that, consequently, he does not fulfill himself in his work but denies himself, has a feeling of misery rather than well-being, does not develop freely his mental and physical energies but is physically exhausted and mentally debased. The worker therefore feels himself at home only during

On the basis of this prior pre-conditioning, monopoly capitalism can play on the passive and individual needs of consumption, can propose ever more complicated and sophisticated modes of satisfaction, develop the need to escape, sell means of forgetting, of distracting oneself from the pressures of industrial organization, means of dreaming that one is human—because there is no chance of actually becoming such—by the acquisition of prefabricated symbols of humanity. And the farther capitalism advances on this road, the more it deadens an already mass-produced and mutilated humanity by means of satisfactions which, while they leave the fundamental dissatisfaction intact, distract one from it; and the more it hopes that these men, preoccupied with ways of escaping and forgetting, will forget to challenge the basis of the whole system, namely the alienation of labor. Capitalism civilizes consumption and leisure in order not to have to civilize social relationships, the relationships of production and of work; it alienates individuals in their work, thereby enabling it to alienate them all the better in their consumption; and inversely, it alienates them in consumption in order to alienate them better in their work.

It is impossible to break out of this vicious circle by maintaining labor struggles on the quantitative level of demands for greater consumption; and inversely it is impossible to challenge the neocapitalist model of consumption (except by invoking very ab-

---

his leisure time, whereas at work he feels homeless. His work is not voluntary but imposed, *forced labor*. It is not satisfaction of a need, but only a *means* for satisfying other needs. . . .

"We arrive at the result that man (the worker) feels himself to be freely active only in his animal functions—eating, drinking and procreating, or at most also in his dwelling and in personal adornment—while in his human functions he is reduced to an animal. The animal becomes human and the human becomes animal.

"Eating, drinking and procreating are of course also genuine human functions. But abstractly considered, apart from the environment of other human activities, and turned into final and sole ends, they are animal functions."—"Economic and Philosophical Manuscripts," translated by T. B. Bottomore, in Erich Fromm, *Marx's Concept of Man* (Ungar, 1961), pp. 98–99.

stractly one or another scale of spiritual values, teeming with medieval and primitivist nostalgia) without attacking the root of "spiritual poverty," namely the alienation of labor.

This task is evidently not simple. The subordination of consumption to production, of all aspects of life to monopoly accumulation, does not provoke a spontaneous revolt. There may even seem to be a circularity: the priorities of the neo-capitalist model of consumption correspond to real needs within the present relationships of production and work, and it may seem impossible to challenge the former until the latter have been transformed.

This circularity is nevertheless more apparent than real. Because the point is not, as Christian ideologists sometimes assert, to begin by reducing the immediate satisfactions which the "consumers' society" promises to alienated workers, and to promise them instead truer satisfactions in the future. The question of the purpose of work, of the model of society, and of consumption, should not be put in the form of an alternative between "frivolous opulence" and "virtuous austerity" but, with reference to immediate demands themselves, in terms of essentially *political* options for the future.

One of the first goals of a political alternative will be to break down the wall which separates the producer from his product and which puts the worker, as mystified consumer, in contradiction with himself as alienated producer. The workers' immediate demands concerning wages, hours, quotas, and qualifications provide the unions, and above all the factory-based sections of the labor parties, with the opportunity to raise the problem of the social and individual utility of the products to which the work is subservient, the question of the value (or worthlessness) of planned innovations, of the real quality of the product, of the orientation which production ought to have in view of felt needs and of the existing scientific and technical potentialities.[13] The

[13] This is not as utopian an affair as it might seem. At the beginning of the 'fifties, the Fiat company experienced a general strike against the production of a new prestige model of automobile, and in favor of the production of tractors and of popular, utility cars. The same remarks, and the same methods, apply evidently to the University (i.e., for the students) with

goal is to succeed in establishing the power of the working class on the level of the company, the industry, and finally of the national economy itself—a power capable of opposing commercial mystifications and the dictates of fashion with an autonomous evaluation of the use value of products, capable of evaluating the real cost, the real rate of profits, and the amount of resources wasted on the level of the company and the overall industry for superfluous or useless research and development. Such power would be capable of opposing the neo-capitalist model of consumption (and of production) with a new order of priorities founded on felt needs, obviously including needs relating to leisure, working conditions, and life style.

Only by reuniting in action and in political unionist thought the producer and the consumer whom capitalism has divided, will the parasitical logic of the system be brought to light, and the rough outlines of a new social model be traced, a model of consumption and of life,[14] in the light of which the model of monopoly capitalism will stand condemned for its absurdity, and will provoke the conscious intention of replacing it.

The positive challenge to neo-capitalist society by a socialist model which indicates positively the human and material possibilities which capitalist development denies, oppresses, and excludes is the only really revolutionary challenge and the only means of making the workers conscious of their stifled needs during this phase of capitalist development where *immediate* needs no longer automatically constitute a revolutionary critique of the system. New revolutionary needs, indeed, do not disappear with the development of productive forces, but are suppressed by social propaganda and preconditioning, deprived of the means of satisfaction and therefore of the means of being made conscious, and cannot be liberated except by dialectical mediation, by the projection of a model which in affirming the possibility of their

---

even greater possibilities for rapid implementation, as witness the recent strike by Italian architecture students who occupied the University buildings, demanding a voice in the determination of their program and of the subjects taught. They won their case.

[14] What Lucio Magri (*loc. cit.*) called proletarian positivity.

satisfaction reveals their existence. This model, while it must necessarily be a total response to capitalism, does not therefore have to be presented as a utopia, nor as a maximalist demand which places socialism beyond capitalism and erects between the two an impenetrable barrier. Quite the opposite: it must present itself as the meaning and the strategic horizon of present struggles and tactical demands. It can exclude neither compromise nor partial objectives, so long as they go in the right direction and as long as that direction is clear. We will return to this subject.

CHAPTER FOUR

The Reproduction of Labor Power: The Model of Consumption

CAN POSITIVE CRITICISM of the capitalist model of development be based on the needs which arise from the development of the productive forces themselves, and on the manner in which so-called affluent capitalist society organizes the satisfaction of these needs?

The question would have no meaning at all if fundamental needs were predetermined once and for all by "human nature." If that were the case, every increase in the production of wealth would mean increasing satisfaction. Finally, absolute satiety could be reached.

Empirical observation shows, on the contrary, that an increase in the standard of living can go hand in hand with an exacerbation of fundamental needs. In France, for instance, the degree to which these needs have remained unsatisfied (poverty as a felt reality) has not diminished from 1950 to 1960, while production has almost doubled. The development of needs has been as fast as (sometimes even faster than) the development of social production; the feeling of poverty has in no way been attenuated by the increase in wealth.[1]

This fact, at first view paradoxical, is often interpreted as indicating the "bourgeoisification" of the working class under the influence of a "civilization of prosperity" and its commercial propaganda: an inextinguishable thirst for enjoyment and comfort is said to have developed in the masses, who now strive to attain the level of "affluence" of the bourgeoisie and middle strata.

This interpretation is at best superficial and tendentious. It ignores the fact that fundamental needs are themselves historical. These needs are conditioned by the development of the means available for their satisfaction. They are conditioned by the development of the techniques of production, that is to say by the development of the nature of work and the conditions of work.

[1] Cf. the statistical inquiry published in *Population*, Winter 1962.

They are conditioned finally by the changes which the development of production techniques brings about in the natural environment, in the (ecological) relation of man to nature. In using up or destroying natural resources (for example, air, space, light, silence), by provoking massive migrations and profound upheavals in the human environment, industrial growth reveals or sharpens certain needs which had not previously been felt.

Thus we must deal with two processes which, at least in the capitalist economy, by no means automatically lead toward a better satisfaction of fundamental needs as a result of increased production:

1. The objects available to satisfy needs increase in quantity, quality, and kind, thus modifying the structure and the nature of direct needs themselves.

2. The conditions of production (the nature of labor) and the social environment are constantly upset by technological development; new means thus become necessary to satisfy direct needs. But production, in a market economy, by no means adjusts automatically to the demand for these new means.

For the sake of clarity, we will examine these two processes separately.

1. *The Superfluous Before the Necessary*

Does the man who eats red meat and white bread, moves with the help of a motor, and dresses in synthetic fibers, live better than the man who eats dark bread and white cheese, moves on a bicycle, and dresses in wool and cotton? The question is almost meaningless. It supposes that in a given society, the same individual has a choice between two different life styles. Practically speaking, this is not the case: only one way of life, more or less rigidly determined, is open to him, and this way of life is conditioned by the structure of production and by its techniques. The latter determine the environment by which needs are conditioned, the objects by which these needs can be satisfied, and the manner of consuming or using these objects.[2]

[2] "Production furnishes consumption not only with its object. It also gives consumption its definition, its character, its finish. . . . The object is

But the basic question is this: what guarantees the adjustment of production to needs, both in general and for a specific product? [3] Liberal economists have long maintained that this adjustment is guaranteed by the mechanism of the market. But this thesis has very few defenders today. Doubtless, if we do not look at the overall picture in optimum human and economic terms, but only at each product taken separately, then we can still maintain that a product totally devoid of use value would not find a buyer. Nevertheless, it is impossible to conclude that the most widely distributed products of mass consumption are really those which at a given stage of technological evolution allow for the best and most rational satisfaction (at the least cost and the least expense of time and trouble) of a given need.

In fact, under capitalism the pursuit of optimum human and economic goals and the pursuit of maximum profit from invested capital coincide only by accident. The pursuit of maximum profit is the first exigency of capital, and the increase of use value is no more than a by-product of this pursuit.

For example, let us take the case of the spread of disposable packaging for milk products. From the viewpoint of use value, the superiority of milk in a cardboard carton or yoghurt in a plastic cup is nil (or negative). From the viewpoint of capitalist enterprise, on the other hand, this substitution is clearly advantageous. The glass bottle or glass jar represented immobilized capital which did not "circulate": empty bottles or jars were recovered

---

not an object as such, but a specific object, which must be consumed in a specific way, a way which is again determined by production itself. Hunger is hunger, but the kind of hunger that is satisfied with cooked meat eaten with a fork and knife is different from the hunger which bolts down raw meat with hand, tooth, and nail. Therefore production produces not only the object of consumption, but also the manner of consumption, not only objectively but also subjectively. Production thus creates the consumer. Production not only furnishes the object of a need, but it also furnishes the need for an object." Marx, *Grundrisse der Kritik der Politischen Oekonomie* (Berlin: Dietz, 1953), p. 14. [Translated from the German by Martin A. Nicolaus.]

[3] Structure of production; order of priorities between, for example, automobiles, housing, and public services. We shall return to this subject.

and reused indefinitely, which entailed the cost of handling, collection, and sterilization. The disposable containers, on the other hand, allow a substantial economy in handling, and permit the profitable sale not only of the dairy product but also of its container. To increase their profits, the big dairy firms thus forced the consumer to purchase a new product at a higher price although its use value remained the same (or diminished).

In other cases, the alternative between maximum profit and maximum use value is even more striking. The Philips trust, for example, perfected fluorescent lighting in 1938. The life of these fluorescent tubes was then 10,000 hours. Production of these tubes would have covered existing needs cheaply and in a relatively short period of time; amortization, on the other hand, would have taken a long time. The invested capital would be recovered slowly, and the labor time necessary to cover existing need would have declined. The company therefore invested additional capital in order to develop fluorescent tubes which burned for only 1,000 hours, in order thus to accelerate the recovery of capital and to realize —at the price of considerable *superfluous* expenditure—a much higher rate of accumulation and of profit.

The same holds true for synthetic fibers, whose durability, for stockings especially, has decreased, and for motor vehicles, which are *deliberately* built with parts which will wear out rapidly (and cost as much as longer-lasting parts would have).[4]

Speaking generally, and regardless of the objective scientific and technical possibilities, technical development in terms of the criteria of maximum profit is often quite different from development in terms of criteria of maximum social and economic utility. Even when fundamental needs remain largely unsatisfied, monopoly capital objectively organizes scarcity, wastes natural resources and human labor, and orients production (and consumption) toward objects whose sale is most profitable, regardless of the need for such objects.[5]

[4] See Vance Packard, *The Waste Makers*, which contains numerous examples of this type.

[5] In 1959 the Canadian government became worried by the fact that the cost of living had risen substantially in the space of a few years, while the

In general, monopoly capitalism tends toward a model of "affluence" which levels consumption "upward": the products offered tend to become standardized by the incorporation of a maximum of "added value" which does not perceptibly increase their use value. At the limit (a limit attained by an impressive range of products), the usefulness of an object becomes the *pretext* for selling superfluous things that are built into the product and multiply its price; the products are sold above all for their packaging and brand names (that is to say, advertising), while their use value becomes a secondary part of the bargain. The packaging and the brand name, moreover, are expressly designed to deceive the buyer as to the quantity, quality, and the nature of the product: tooth paste is endowed with erotic virtues, detergents with magic qualities, the automobile (in the U.S.) is extolled as a status symbol.

The apparent diversity of the products badly masks their true uniformity: the difference between brands is marginal. All American automobiles are identical with regard to the incorporation of a maximum of "packaging" and false luxury, to the point where an intense advertising campaign is necessary to "educate" the consumer, from school age on, to perceive the differences in detail and not to perceive the substantial similarities.[6] This dictatorship of the monopolies over needs and individual tastes was broken in the United States only from the outside, by the producers of European automobiles. "Upward" leveling, that is, leveling toward the incorporation of a maximum of superfluity, has been carried out in this instance to the detriment of the use value of the product, whose consumers were unable for years to reverse the tendency of an

price of agricultural and industrial products had remained stable. An investigating committee blamed the spread of supermarkets: after having eliminated independent grocery stores, the supermarkets (often linked to the monopolies of the food industry) established uniformly high prices. Above all, in order to extract the maximum profit per square foot of display area, they pushed the sale of expensive, luxuriously packaged products, to the detriment of products which have the same use value but are less costly.

[6] See David Riesman, *The Lonely Crowd* (Yale University Press, 1950). See also Ernest Mandel, *Traité d'Economie Marxiste*, Vol. II, Chapter XVII, pp. 354–359 (Julliard, 1962).

oligopoly to sell goods of a diminishing use value at a constantly increasing price.

The pursuit of maximum profit, to continue with this example of one of the pilot industries of the most developed country, was not even accompanied by scientific and technological fertility. The tendency to prefer the accessory to the essential, the improvement of the profit rate to the improvement of use value, has resulted in *absolute* wastage. None of the four major post-war technical innovations in automobile design: disc brakes, fuel injection, hydro-pneumatic suspension, rotating piston, originated in the American car industry—an industry which with every annual model change brings into conflict the two biggest manufacturing groups in the world. They compete mainly for maximum productivity, not for maximum use value. The notion that competition would be a factor in accelerating technical and scientific progress is thus, in large part, a myth. Competition does not contribute to technical progress unless such progress allows for the growth of profits. Technical progress, in other words, is essentially concentrated on productivity, and only incidentally on the pursuit of a human optimum in the manner of production and in the manner of consumption.

This is why, in all developed capitalist societies, gigantic waste coexists with largely unsatisfied fundamental needs (needs for housing, medical care, education, hygiene, etc.). This is also why the claim that capitalist profit (distributed or consumed) does not represent a great burden for the economy (about five per cent of the French national revenue) is a gross myth.[7]

Certainly the confiscation of the surplus value consumed by the capitalists would not result in a perceptible improvement of the condition of the people or the workers. But nobody claims any longer that in order to transform society the principal attack must be leveled against the profits pocketed by individual capitalists, against the incomes of the great families and the major employers.

[7] This myth is contained in the work of J. Fourastié, *Pourquoi Nous Travaillons*, Collection "Que Sais-je?" (Presses Universitaires de France, 1962).

What must be attacked is not the personal incomes created by capitalist profits; it is rather the orientation which the system and the logic of profit, that is to say of capitalist accumulation, impress on the economy and the society as a whole; it is the capitalist control over the apparatus of production and the resulting inversion of real priorities in the model of consumption.

What must be constantly exposed and denounced is this organized waste of labor and resources on the one hand and this organized scarcity (scarcity of time, air, of collective services and cultural possibilities) on the other hand. On the level of the model of consumption, this combination of waste and scarcity is the major absurdity of the capitalist system. To attack the great families and the profits they make (in money terms) is always less effective than challenging the capitalist control and management over individual companies and the economy as a whole in the name of a different policy, that is to say in the name of an orientation of production to needs and not to greater profits. To show the possibility of this policy and the different results to which it would lead, to outline a *different* model of consumption, is of a much more real and revolutionary significance than all the abstract speeches about the billions pocketed by monopolies and about the need to nationalize them. Nationalization of the monopolies will not be a mobilizing goal unless linked to a concrete program which demonstrates why they must be nationalized, what presently unattainable results such nationalization will have, and what nationalization can and should change.

2. *The Social Cost of Private Initiative*

The effects of capitalist production on the environment and on society are a second source of waste and of distortion. In fact, what was said about the capitalist control over industry holds true *a fortiori* for the orientation of the economy in general. The most profitable production for each entrepreneur is not necessarily the most advantageous one for the consumers; the pursuit of maximum profit and the pursuit of optimum use value do not coincide when each product is considered separately. But if instead of considering the action of each entrepreneur (in fact of each oligopoly) separately, we consider the resulting total of all such actions and their repercussions on society, then we note an even sharper contradiction between this overall result and the social and economic optimum.

This contradiction results essentially from the limits which the criteria of profitability impose on capitalist initiative. According to the logic of this initiative, the most profitable activities are the most important ones, and activities whose product or result cannot be measured according to the criteria of profitability and return are neglected or abandoned to decay. These non-profitable activities, whose desirability cannot even be understood in capitalist terms, consist of all those investments which cannot result in production for the market under the given social and political circumstances, that is to say, which do not result in a commercial exchange comprising the profitable sale of goods and services. In fact this category includes all investments and services which answer to human needs that cannot be expressed in market terms as demands for salable commodities: the need for education, city planning, cultural and recreational facilities, works of art, research, public health, public transportation (and also economic planning, reforestation, elimination of water- and air-pollution, noise control, etc.)—in short, all economic activities which belong to the "public domain" and cannot arise or survive except as public services, regardless of their profitability.

The demand for the satisfaction of these needs, which cannot be expressed in market terms, necessarily takes on political and collective forms; and the satisfaction of these collective needs, precisely because it cannot be procured except by public services belonging to the collectivity, constitutes a permanent challenge to the laws and the spirit of the capitalist system. In other words, there is a whole sphere of fundamental, priority needs which constitute an objective challenge to capitalist logic. Only socialism can recognize the priority nature and assure the priority satisfaction of these needs. This does not mean that we must await the establishment of socialism or fight for socialism only by political campaigning. It means rather that the existence of this sphere of collective needs now offers the socialist forces the chance to demand and to achieve, in the name of these needs, the creation and the development of a sphere of services, a sphere which represents a popular victory and constitutes a permanent antagonism to the capitalist system and permanently restricts its functioning. We shall return to this point later.

The acuteness of this antagonism—and the sharpness of the contradiction between capitalist initiative and collective needs—necessarily grows. It grows principally as a result of the fact that collective needs and the cost of their satisfaction are not in principle included in the cost of capitalist decisions and initiatives. There is a disjunction between the direct cost of the productive investment for the private investor, and the indirect, social cost which this investment creates to cover the resulting collective needs, such as housing, roads, the supply of energy and water; in short, the infrastructure. There is also a disjunction between the computation of direct production costs by the private investor and the social cost which his investment will bring with it: for example, expenses for education, housing, transportation, various services; in short, the entrepreneur's criteria of profitability, which measure the desirability of the investment, and the criteria of human and collective desirability, are not identical. As a consequence, the collective needs engendered by capitalist investment are covered haphazardly or not at all; the satisfaction of these needs is neglected or subordinated to more profitable "priorities" because these needs were not foreseen and included in advance in the total cost of the project.

Thus, when a capitalist group decides to invest in a given project and a given locality, it need not bother to ask itself what degree of priority its project has in the scale of needs, what social costs it will entail, what social needs it will engender, what long term public investments it will make necessary later on, or what alternatives its private decision will render impossible. The decision of the capitalist group will be guided rather by the existing market demand, the available facilities and equipment, and the proximity of the market and the sources of raw materials.

The first result of this situation is that the decision of a private trust to invest does not in most cases have any but an accidental relationship to the real but non-marketable needs of the local, regional, or national unit: the model of development which monopoly capitalism imposes on insufficiently developed regions is as a general rule a colonial model. The balanced development of Brittany or Southern Italy, for example, if it were to answer real needs would in the first place demand investments to revive agricultural productivity, to assure local processing of raw materials, and to occupy the underemployed population in industries having local outlets. Priority thus would have to be given to educational and cultural services, to food and agricultural industries, to light industry, chemical and pharmaceutical manufacturing, to communication and transportation. If these priorities were chosen, the local communities could develop toward a diversification of their activities, toward a relative economic, cultural, and social autonomy, toward a fuller development of social relations and exchanges, and thus toward a fuller development of human relations and abilities.

Capitalist initiative functions only in terms of the existing *market* demand. If there is no such demand in the underdeveloped regions for the products capable of bringing about balanced development, then capitalist initiative will consist of setting up export industries in these regions. The resulting type of development, besides being very limited, will reverse the real priorities: the under-employed local manpower will be drained toward assembly workshops (although not to the extent of providing full employment), toward satellite factories which are sub-contractors of distant trusts, and toward the production or extraction of raw materials or of individual components which will be transformed or assembled elsewhere.

The local community, instead of being raised toward a new, richer internal equilibrium, will thus be practically destroyed by having a new element of imbalance grafted onto its already out-of-date structures: agriculture, instead of being made healthier and richer, will be ruined by the exodus of manpower and the land will be abandoned; the local industries, instead of being diversified in terms of local needs, will undergo specialization and impoverishment; local or regional autonomy, instead of being reinforced, will be diminished even more, since the centers of decision making for the local activities are in Paris or Milan and the new local industries are the first to suffer the shock of economic fluctuations: the quality of the local community's social relations, instead of being improved, will be impoverished; local manpower will get the dirtiest and the most monotonous jobs; the ancient towns (*bourgs*) will become dormitory cities with new cafés and juke boxes in place of cultural facilities; the former civilization will be destroyed and replaced by nothing; those of the new workers who do not travel one, two, or even three hours daily by bus to go to and from their work will be penned up in concrete cages or in shanty towns: in the mother country as well as in the colonies there is a process of "slummification" ("*clochardisation*"). The colonies, at least, can free themselves of foreign colonialism; the underdeveloped regions in the mother country, however, are often irreversibly colonized and deprived of independent livelihood by monopoly capitalism, or even emptied of their population and turned into a wasteland.

The drift of industry toward the underdeveloped regions, in the conditions which have just been described, cannot really be compared to an industrialization of these areas. It tends rather to destroy all possibility of balance between the city and the countryside by the creation of new, giant agglomerations which empty the back country. The small peasants will not be able to rationalize their methods (that would require a policy of credit and equipment favoring cooperative or collective modes of farming); instead they will sell their holdings to the benefit of the agrarian capitalists. The former peasants will install themselves as shop keepers, café owners, or unskilled laborers in the new big city or in the capital. The drift of certain industries toward less developed regions is therefore not at all comparable to decentralization. On the contrary, it is only a marginal phenomenon of industry's tendency to concentrate geographically. Industry is attracted by industry, money by money. Both go by preference where markets and conditions of profitability already exist, not where these must first be created. Thus regional disparities tend to grow.

The principal cause of geographic concentration of industry has been the public prefinancing, during the past decades, of the social bases of industrial expansion in the highly dense zones: housing, transportation, trained manpower, infrastructure. Now, the savings realized by individual industries due to geographic concentration are an extra burden for the collectivity. After a certain point has been reached the operating costs of the large cities grow dizzily (long traveling time, air pollution, noise, lack of space, etc.). The overpopulation of the urban centers has as a counterpart the depopulation of non-developed areas below the threshold of economic and social viability, their economic and human impoverishment, and the obliteration of their potential; and the cost of the social reproduction of labor power is multiplied. (For a further discussion of this subject, see Part Two.)

This double process of congestion and decline has one and the same root: the concentration of economic power in a small number of monopolistic groups which drain off a large part of the economic surplus realized in production and distribution and which reinvest that surplus where conditions of immediate profitability are already present. Therefore the resources available for a regional and social policy consonant with real needs are always insufficient, especially because monopoly competition engenders new consumer needs and new collective expenses which are incompatible with a government policy aimed at balanced development.

The costs of infrastructure (roads, transportation, city maintenance and planning, provision of energy and water) which monopoly expansion imposes on the collectivity as it spreads (namely in the congested zones), in practice make it impossible to provide such services in the areas where the need is greatest: the billions swallowed up by the great cities are in the last analysis diverted from economically and humanly more advantageous uses.

Furthermore, the cost of the infrastructure, which the orientation given by monopoly capitalism to consumption demands, represents an obstacle to the satisfaction of priority needs. The most striking example in this regard is that of the automobile industry. For the production of a means of evasion and escape, this industry has diverted productive resources, labor, and capital from priority tasks such as housing, education, public transportation, public health, city planning, and rural services. The priority given by monopoly capitalism to the automobile gets stronger and stronger: city planning must be subordinated to the requirements of the automobile, roads are built instead of houses (this is very clear in Italy, for example), and public transportation is sacrificed.

And finally the private automobile becomes a social necessity: urban space is organized in terms of private transportation; public transportation lags farther and farther behind the spread of the suburbs and the increasing distance required to travel to work; the pedestrian or the cyclist becomes a danger to others and himself; athletic and cultural facilities are removed from the city, beyond the reach of the non-motorized suburbanite and often even of the city dweller. The possession of an automobile becomes a basic necessity because the universe is organized in terms of private transportation. This process is halted only with difficulty in the advanced capitalist countries. To the extent that the indispensability of private automobiles has made life unbearable in the large, overpopulated cities where air, light, and space are lacking, motorized escape will continue to be an important—although decreasing—element in the reproduction of labor power, even when priority has returned to city planning, to collective services, and to public transportation.

3. *Collective Needs*

Monopoly expansion thus not only creates new needs by throwing onto the market mass consumption products symbolizing an alleged comfort which becomes a need because it is available; it creates needs by modifying the conditions under which labor power can be reproduced. In point of fact, the development of needs in capitalist society often results less from the improvement and the enrichment of human faculties than from an increase in the harshness of the material environment, from a deterioration in living conditions, from the necessity for more complex and more costly instruments to satisfy fundamental needs, to reproduce labor power.[8]

The Marxist distinction between fundamental and historical needs thus becomes problematical and risks creating confusion in all cases where because of man's destruction or distortion of nature fundamental needs can no longer be satisfied—or even apprehended—except in a mediate manner. Between the natural origin of a need and its natural object, we note the interposition of instruments which not only are human products, but which are essentially social products. After the destruction of the natural environment and its replacement by a social environment, fundamental needs can only be satisfied in a social manner: they become immediately social needs; or, more exactly, fundamental needs mediated by society.

This is true, for example, of the need for air, which is immediately apprehended as the need for vacations, for public gardens, for city planning, for escape from the city; of the need for nightly rest, for physical and mental relaxation, which becomes the need for tasteful, comfortable housing protected against noise; of the need to eat, which in the large industrial cities becomes the need for food which can be consumed immediately after a day of work —that is, the need for cafeterias, restaurants, canned foods, and foods that require a minimum of preparation time; of the need for cleanliness, which in the absence of sunlight and natural beaches or rivers becomes the need for hygienic facilities, laundries, or washing machines, and so on.

In all these examples, the historical form which the fundamental need assumes cannot be confused with the historical need as such: the need in question is not a new and "rich" need which corresponds to an enrichment of man and a development of his faculties; it is merely an eternal biological need which now demands "rich" means of satisfaction because the natural environment has become impoverished, because there has been impover-

[8] On the quantitative and qualitative increase of expended energy, and the means necessary to reproduce it, see Pierrette Sartin, *La fatigue industrielle* (Paris: Sadot, 1960).

ishment of man's relation to nature, exhaustion or destruction of resources (air, water, light, silence, space) which until now were taken as natural.

Now the nature of capitalist society is to constrain the individual to buy back individually, as a consumer, the means of satisfaction of which the society has socially deprived him. The capitalist trust appropriates or uses up air, light, space, water, and (by producing dirt and noise) cleanliness and silence gratuitously or at a preferential price; contractors, speculators, and merchants then resell all of these resources to the highest bidder. The destruction of natural resources has been social; the reproduction of these vitally necessary resources is social in its turn. But even though the satisfaction of the most elementary needs now must pass through the mediation of social production, service, and exchange, no social initiative assures or foresees the replacement of what has been destroyed, the social reparation of the spoliation which individuals have suffered. On the contrary, once its social repercussions and its inverted priorities have aggravated the conditions in which social individuals exist, private enterprise then exploits at a profit the greater needs of these same social individuals. It is they as individual consumers who will have to pay for the growth of the social cost of the reproduction of their labor power, a cost which often surpasses their means.

The workers understand the scandal inherent in this situation in a direct and confused manner. The capitalist trust, after having exploited them and mutilated them *in* their work, comes to exploit them and mutilate them *outside* of their work. It imposes on them, for example, the cost, the fatigue, and the long hours lost on public transportation; it imposes on them the search for and the price of housing, made scarce by the trust's manpower needs and made more expensive by the speculations which increasing scarcity produces.

The same thing holds for air, light, cleanliness, and hygiene, whose price becomes prohibitive. For example, great industrial concentration forces women to go to work for pay, because one paycheck in the family is not enough to buy the means necessary for the reproduction of labor power[9] in the big city. In the absence of public services, the mechanization of housework becomes a necessity: washing machines, refrigerators, ready-to-eat foods, semi-automatic stoves, and restaurants come to be a necessity. But the satisfaction of this need, even though it has its origin in the condition of social production and of social life, is left to private enterprise, which profits from it. Individuals have to pay for this satisfaction, so that a very important part of a working woman's wages which once were (wrongly) considered as "supplemental" income, serves only to cover the supplementary expenses which women's work entails.[10]

On the level of collective needs, and only on this level, the theory of impoverishment thus continues to be valid. The social cost of the reproduction of labor power (the simple reproduction, and as we shall show below, the wider reproduction) tends to rise as fast as or faster than individual purchasing power; the workers' social standard of living tends to stagnate, to worsen, even if their individual standard of living (expressed in terms of monetary purchasing power) rises. And it is extremely difficult, if not impossible, for urban workers to obtain a qualitative improvement in their living standard as a result of a raise in their direct wages within

[9] Labor power, according to Marx, is the quantity of productive energy expended by a worker during the process of work. In order to keep on working day after day, he must constantly reproduce his labor power; that is, he must eat, rest, sleep, keep healthy, etc. Similarly, the working class as a whole must be constantly reproduced: workers must raise children to replace them when they are old, and skills must be passed on from generation to generation. In the present volume, the phrase, "simple reproduction of labor power" generally refers to all the means necessary to reproduce and maintain labor power as of now; while "wider reproduction" refers to the totality of vocational training programs, educational institutions, public information media, and cultural facilities necessary to maintain and reproduce over time the sort of educated working force and administrative personnel required by a complex society whose technology and knowledge evolve at an ever-quickening pace. See Karl Marx, *Capital,* Vol. 1, Ch. 4, Sec. 3. [Translators' note.]

[10] See Geneviève Rocard, "Sur le travail des femmes mariées," *Les Temps Modernes,* September–October 1962.

the framework of capitalist structures. It is this quasi-impossibility which gives demands in the name of collective needs a revolutionary significance.

The nature of collective needs, in effect, is that they often cannot be expressed in terms of monetary demands. They involve a set of collective resources, services, and facilities which escape the law of the market, capitalist initiative, and all criteria of profitability. These needs, inexpressible in economic terms, are at least virtually in permanent contradiction to capitalism and mark the limit of its effectiveness. These are the needs which capitalism tends to neglect or to suppress, insofar as capitalism knows only the *homo œconomicus*—defined by the consumption of merchandise and its production—and not the human man, the consumer, producer, and user of goods which cannot be sold, bought, or reproduced. It is these needs which, although they are basically biological, all have a necessarily cultural and at least potentially creative dimension, due to the destruction by industry of a natural environment for which human praxis[11] must substitute a new social environment and civilization.

Among these needs are:

—Housing and city planning, not only in quantitative but in qualitative terms as well. An urban esthetic and an urban landscape, an environment which furthers the development of human faculties instead of debasing them, must be recreated. Now it is

[11] The word "praxis" is used here in its original Greek sense as rehabilitated by Sartre (in his *Critique of Dialectical Reason*) and other Marxian philosophers. It means "activity" in a very strong sense. The praxis of an individual, a group, or a society is the action or totality of actions that change Nature ("physis," in Greek) in accordance with human needs, and that produce or create an "unnatural" order ("anti-physis") whose existence rests solely on human activity, on a constant struggle against and conquest of Nature.

The material results of human praxis may of course appear to be some external or anti-human force against which individuals are powerless and that crushes them: for instance, the process of production, the seemingly blind forces of the business cycle, the "iron laws" of economics. Whenever individuals meet the overall result of their praxes as an external and hostile process, their praxis is "alienated" and its result "estranged."

obvious that it is not profitable to provide 200 square feet of green area per inhabitant, to plan parks, roads, and squares. The application of the law of the market leads, on the contrary, to reserve the best living conditions for the privileged, who need them least, and to deny them to the workers who, because they do the most difficult and the lowest-paid work, need them profoundly.[12] The workings of this law also push the workers farther and farther from their place of work, and impose on them additional expense and fatigue.

—Collective services, such as public transportation, laundries and cleaners, child day care centers and nursery schools. These are non-profitable in essence: for in terms of profit, it is necessarily more advantageous to sell individual vehicles, washing machines, and magical soap powders. And since these services are most needed by those who have the lowest incomes, their expansion on a commercial basis presents no interest at all for capital. Only public services can fill the need.

—Collective cultural, athletic, and health facilities: schools, theatres, libraries, concert halls, swimming pools, stadiums, hospitals, in short, all the facilities necessary for the reestablishment of physical and intellectual balance for the development of human faculties. The non-profitability of these facilities is evident, as is their extreme scarcity (and usually great cost) in almost all of the capitalist countries.

—Balanced regional development in terms of optimum economic and human criteria, which we have already contrasted to neo-colonialist "slummification."

—Information, communication, active group leisure. Capital-

[12] Under these circumstances the law of the market presents this additional absurdity: it makes the price of scarce resources like space, air, light, and silence rise dizzily, when by nature these resources *cannot be reproduced*. The seller of these resources, however high a price he gets for them, has had no hand in their creation and is perfectly incapable of reproducing them. The sale and purchase of these resources is a pure and simple act of spoliation committed on the collectivity. Their socialization, that is to say their control and social allocation in terms of the simple criteria of need, is a fundamental demand.

ism not only does not have any interest in these needs,[13] it tends even to suppress them. The commercial dictatorship of the monopolies cannot in fact function without a mass of passive consumers, separated by place and style of living, incapable of getting together and communicating directly, incapable of defining together their specific needs (relative to their work and life situation), their preoccupations, their outlook on society and the world—in short, their common project. Mass pseudo-culture, while producing passive and stupefying entertainments, amusements, and pastimes, does not and cannot satisfy the needs arising out of dispersion, solitude, and boredom. This pseudo-culture is less a consequence than a cause of the passivity and the impotence of the individual in a mass society. It is a device invented by monopoly capital to facilitate its dictatorship over a mystified, docile, debased humanity, whose impulses of real violence must be redirected into imaginary channels.

4. *Toward an Alternative Model*

Collective needs are thus objectively in contradiction to the logic of capitalist development. This development is by nature incapable of giving them the degree of priority which they warrant.[14] This is why demands in the name of collective needs imply a radical challenge of the capitalist system, on the economic, political, and cultural levels.

From the economic point of view (as we have already said), the mechanism of capitalist accumulation automatically tends to give a high degree of priority to individual market needs, into which, because they are considered as the principal motive force of expansion, all collective needs are translated. The subordinate

[13] All information media show a deficit; only advertising, that is to say the sale of commercial "information" which they are paid to sell, allows some of them to balance their budgets.

[14] Sweden is no exception to the rule, although the underdevelopment of collective facilities, compared with individual and private equipment, is less dramatic than elsewhere in certain respects. The official ideology of Sweden, indeed, implies that alienation of work must be accepted and that the worker must look for his freedom in private life and private consumption.

position of collective needs is even more evident in a highly developed capitalist economy such as the American or British, where a gigantic apparatus of commercial propaganda resorts to ever more perfected psychological tricks in order to excite and stimulate individual needs, while only isolated voices or bureaucratic apparatuses speak for collective needs. The attempt to counterbalance the dictatorship of monopoly capital over the means of information and individual education has always been ineffective because of the disproportion of forces: it is practically impossible for organs of information and education to fight against commercial propaganda so long, at least, as they address a dispersed and atomized public.

This practical impossibility is obviously due to the fact that collective needs can not be substantially defined except collectively. For it is impossible for any individual to obtain satisfaction of those needs which he feels (according to Marx's distinction) as a "social individual" rather than as an "accidental individual." Left to himself, he will always tend to demand individual goods rather than collective services or facilities—to demand, in other words, a "market economy" and a "society of consumption" rather than an economy and a society founded on service. This is for the simple reason that he has some chance of someday obtaining a washing machine, a car, and the necessary wage increase; but as an "accidental individual" he has no chance of obtaining public laundry service, rapid and comfortable means of public transportation, parks and athletic facilities ten minutes from his home, or even suitable housing at a price he can afford.

The preference for the priorities and the values of the "society of consumption" for the ideology of mature capitalism is therefore not spontaneous; it arises out of the individuals' powerlessness to define and to prefer something else. Thus is created the spontaneous primacy of demands for greater consumption, demands in which the bourgeoisie joyfully thinks it recognizes the striving for a life in the bourgeois image: the working class is "becoming bourgeois," and even in its demands it seems to endorse the values of capitalist civilization. It seems to confirm that the acquisition and the enjoyment of private goods is the supreme goal of "man"; it seems to be caught in the trap of the merchants of pseudo-culture and of alleged affluence; it seems to demonstrate that needs and desires can be shaped by monopolistic production in terms of its own greatest profit.

The only thing that can be effective in destroying these myths is the outline of a social model of consumption—a way of life and a culture based on social service, on free communication and free time, on the satisfaction of cultural or creative needs, on the full development of human faculties. It is not enough to say that this model (which does not yet exist anywhere) must be socialist, that socialism means the subordination of the purpose and methods of production to human needs and development. It is necessary again to define the concrete substance of collective needs at their roots, and to give the certainty that satisfaction is not impossible. This can only be done in common by mass political and labor organization and action, by organizing and grouping individuals where their collective needs are experienced, by making them acquire a common consciousness of their common needs, at work and at home, and by defining with them the common goals of common actions, of mass demonstrations and of strikes.[15]

Even this is no more than a beginning. The process set in motion by mass action shall not culminate in an electoral campaign on the theme of "The sky over the Ruhr must become blue again." [16] If it is to be effective, this process must challenge the model and mechanism of capitalist accumulation in the name of a society based on public service; it must lead up to demanding that the investment function be socialized, that planning be democratized according to a scale of fundamental priorities which reflect needs and not the projections of past monopoly expansion. More concretely, and as a first step, there must be a struggle to make the capitalist trusts pay for the collective services and facilities

[15] Strikes and demonstrations for public housing and for better transportation services were successfully carried out in the large Italian cities, along with huge region-wide meetings to demand regional development programs.

[16] Anti-air-pollution campaign slogan of Willi Brandt, leader of the Social Democratic Party, during the West German legislative elections in 1961.

which their activity renders necessary, services which are an integral part of the social cost of production and must be under the control and management of the workers.

The social model of the phase of transition toward socialism, and the superiority of socialism over capitalism, will emerge more concretely in the course of these struggles. And the partial victories won in this way, if they improve living conditions, will not thereby reinforce capitalism. On the contrary: the public expropriation of real estate, the socialization of housing construction, free medicine, the nationalization of the pharmaceutical industry, public cleaning and transportation services, an increase in collective facilities, regional development planning (elaborated and executed under the control of local assemblies and financed by public funds), and the *social control* of all these sectors which are necessarily outside of the criteria of profit—these things weaken and counteract the capitalist system from within. Their mere functioning as social services requires a constant struggle against the capitalist system itself, since they canot be kept working without a form of social control over the whole process of capitalist accumulation and the latter's subordination to a democratically determined scale of priorities reflecting the scale of needs.

Expansion of the socialized sector, or the satisfactory operation of the already existing social services, can be obtained only by continually restricting the private sector, by increasingly limiting its "freedom" to produce and invest. The only way the socialized sector can survive is by limiting capital's sphere of autonomy and counteracting its logic, by restraining its field of action, and bringing its potential centers of accumulation under social control. The socialized sector must take control of the industries it depends upon (socialized medicine must control the pharmaceutical industry, social housing construction must control the building industry, for example), or else it will be nibbled away and exploited by the private sector, as has happened in France.

The defense of the socialized sector requires its expansion; and the functioning of the socialized sector demands that the private centers of capital accumulation (industrial and financial monopolies) be subordinated to it and placed under social control.[17] This is why, far from stabilizing, "humanizing" or "socializing" capitalism, the socialized sector is a permanent contradiction in its midst. The bourgeoisie knows this well, often better than the working class movement. This contradiction can only sharpen with time, and at the same time sharpen the class conflicts, until one or the other sector succumbs to the final assault (which can, in the best of hypotheses, be peaceful) after successive partial setbacks.

It is on this dialectical progression that the so-called strategy of intermediate goals and of peaceful transition toward socialism is based. But none of these partial goals, no partial socialization of the economy, no partial power to the working class, nor the sum of partial victories, will in itself constitute the revolution. We are not advocating a "nibbling" tactic, a strategy of "progressively investing" the centers of power through a war of siege and endurance. On the contrary, no partial conquest nor the sum of such conquests will ever lead to a miraculous "qualitative leap," nor will they ever make capitalism tilt toward socialism as a drop of water makes a vase overflow. If the strategy of intermediate goals is trapped by this illusion, it will fully deserve the labels of reformist and social-democrat which its critics give it.

The intermediate goals and the structural reforms which they demand constitute a strategy, and escape their reabsorption by capitalism only if they present themselves from the beginning as successive approximations and stages toward a socialist society which is their meaning: a meaning which must be illustrated and made concrete at each stage, a meaning in the light of which each intermediate goal must appear as progressing toward new conquests, or else all past victories become fruitless.

The struggle for the expansion of social control and the expansion of the socialized sector will sharpen the contradictions and

[17] The example of the French social security system furnishes a sad illustration of this fact, since this institution uses the wage earners' money not only to finance the benefits which they receive, but also most hospital and sanitary equipment, and all the profits of a Malthusian pharmaceutical industry, itself a source of appreciable profits for the chemical trusts.

deepen the crisis of capitalism only if these objectives are seen not as ends but as means (which are in fact also ends, but only provisionally) which prefigure what socialist society can and should be. It is in this way that each battle will prepare and announce new ones, will elevate the level of consciousness and of struggle, will anchor the socialist project in the feelings of the masses and will persuade them to defend the past conquests by future, broader conquests. This presupposes, obviously, that the leaders have an overall perspective; it presupposes the elaboration of an "overall alternative" to capitalism, from which each victory receives its meaning. The advance toward socialism will be made in this way or not made at all.

If the overall perspective is lacking, then the sum of all reforms, however advanced they may be, will be reabsorbed by capitalism, resulting in a "mixed economy" of the Scandinavian type in which the power of capital and alienated labor survive while "welfare" is given to all.

If, on the other hand, mediations between the overall goal and everyday action are lacking, then in the absence of intermediate goals capable of making the ultimate goal and the road toward it concrete, socialism will remain an abstract idea, an idea in the name of which dogmatic extremists will reject all structural reforms that indeed are not yet socialism in themselves, while indulging, under the cover of revolutionary phraseology, in fruitless, visionless, and primitive rear guard actions.

CHAPTER FIVE

The Wider Reproduction of Labor Power: The Model of Civilization

UP TO NOW we have argued only from the viewpoint of fundamental needs. We have rediscovered these needs in other needs which are often mistakenly considered "affluent." We have shown that these new needs, far from indicating satiety and the transition to a higher level of civilization, are often nothing more than the search for the means of satisfying a fundamental need within the context of the modern industrial city.[1]

But it is impossible to let the matter rest there. Even when they constitute the underlying reality of historical needs, the fundamental needs of today are no longer the same as those of one hundred or even only twenty-five years ago. To say that a need can no longer be satisfied without the mediation of social production is to say that needs have become increasingly emancipated from the natural sphere. The need is no longer only for a natural resource which can be taken at will, but for a social product which presupposes a certain type of collaboration between individuals and which determines their relationship to society and to nature. Every need is in fact socially determined: it cannot hope to be satisfied except through social mediation; from beginning to end it is the need for a certain social organization.

But this means also that all fundamental needs now have a cultural dimension, both on the level of consumption and on the level of the production of their object. Hunger is from the beginning hunger for food which has been produced, transported, and prepared by others, cooked with the help of instruments made by others, and eaten in the company of others: hunger is the need for food and at the same time the need for interchanges and relationships with others. Likewise, the labor power expended in social production is not simply a homogeneous quantity of organic

[1] See Laura Conti's concept of "historico-fundamental" needs, *Les Temps Modernes*, October 1963.

energy which must be reconstituted by the consumption of goods and services; it is also from the beginning a socially conditioned force, a force which the individual does not derive directly from his contacts with nature and does not apply directly to nature: he derives it from (and applies it to) social collaboration with others, and he furnishes it as a capital of ability, knowledge, and experience accumulated during a social process of upbringing, education, research, and communication. And this labor power is worthless in itself except insofar as it articulates with the labor power of others in social recognition, collaboration, and interchange.

This recognition and interchange inevitably remain under the domination of economic categories so long as the scarcity of the goods necessary for existence is acute. Social collaboration is then ruled by the necessity of rationing scarce resources in order to be able to produce them in greater quantity. Whatever form this rationing may take (authoritarian distribution or money rationing), labor power remains rigorously subject to the laws of accumulation, a socio-economic imperative which surpasses the individual, confronts him as the constraint exercised by all over each one, and remains alien to him.

The interest of society and the interest or need of the individual are necessarily different so long as scarcity is severe; the individual then is non-essential, and production (or accumulation) is essential. It is then not a question of realizing oneself in societal work but of sacrificing oneself in it, of serving production through it. The socialist morality of the period of primary accumulation in its own way reflects this situation with its corresponding necessity for an authoritarian society: man is a means of producing machines, and before becoming "the most precious capital," man is among all machines the least valuable because the least scarce.

1. "*Human Capital*"

However, when the production of life—that is, of the goods necessary to existence—is a virtually solved problem, then the problem becomes that of the kind and content of the life to be produced: the circle of "living in order to work and working in order to live" is no longer closed. The subordination of individuals to society as to an alien command ceases to be absolutely necessary; their subordination to production even leads to absurdities such as the waste and overproduction of "wealth" whose multiplication is still required by the logic of the system of accumulation, even though it no longer corresponds to human needs.[2]

This impasse has a clear lesson; on the level of production it gives rise to a demand which no longer arises out of economic necessity itself; the human demand for the subordination of production to needs. This exigency makes itself felt among the agents of production in the form of doubt, perplexity, vague discontent, or, in the best cases, as revolt against the sense or nonsense of productive activity. Why live only in order to produce? Why produce if the things produced and the manner in which they are produced do not produce men and a life which are ends unto themselves?

This exigency is born out of praxis itself, the moment the latter becomes conscious of itself. And praxis becomes conscious of itself from the moment when, no longer harassed by acute scarcity, it ceases to understand itself only as expenditure of energy, as sweat, and begins to grasp itself as free and creative activity, as reciprocal interrelationship, as potential mastery; in short, when praxis sees itself as its own end.

From that point on a conflict which is most often latent, but overt and severe in an increasing number of areas, begins to oppose the most qualified workers to the logic of monopoly capitalism. When Alsthom takes control and changes the management of Neyrpic, when an incoherent policy condemns a mining region to slow death, when SNECMA, Nord-Aviation or Thomson-

[2] It makes little difference, incidentally, whether the system of accumulation is capitalist or socialist. Even in socialist societies the subordination of individuals to production ultimately leads to overproduction and waste. Waste is not only due to the exploitation of labor, that is, to the private appropriation of surplus value. In effect, exploitation has been abolished in socialist society, but not accumulation as an end in itself. That is why the problem of unsalable surpluses arises, that is, the problem of adjusting production to need, especially in Czechoslovakia. And this problem cannot be resolved in economic terms. The questions of knowing *what* to produce, and how, cannot be answered except by the individuals themselves.

Houston see their activity decline and their programs cut off, when Bull [3] undergoes a crisis and threatens to fall into the hands of an American trust, when Air France deliberately hands over to private companies its profitable lines, then the technicians and engineers are likely to enter the battle. In order to defend their careers? They could pursue their careers elsewhere; many among them could get better pay by changing companies. In order to defend the old management for which (at Neyrpic, for example) they often felt sympathy? So it sometimes appears. But in reality the contradiction which leads them to revolt is not only the contradiction between management by independent owners and management by a trust remote controlled by a bank or a holding company.

The fundamental contradiction is that between the requirements and criteria of profitability set by monopoly capital and the big banks on the one hand, and on the other the inherent requirements of an autonomous, creative activity which is an end in itself: an activity which measures the scientific and technical potential of an enterprise in scientific and technical terms and which sees this "technological capital," this "human capital"—the cooperation of polished teamwork, the possibility of conquering new

[3] *Alsthom, Société Générale de Constructions électriques et mécaniques S.A.*, is an electrical and mechanical engineering firm.

Etablissement Neyrpic is a firm of mechanical engineers, specializing in the manufacture of turbines and hydraulic machinery.

SNECMA (*Société Nationale d'Etudes et de Constructions de Moteurs d'Aviation*), National Company for the Study and Construction of Airplane Motors, is a nationalized concern which was established in May 1945 to replace the *Société des Moteurs Gnôme et Rhône*, which had been accused of collaboration with the Nazis.

Nord-Aviation, Société Nationale de Construction Aéronautique, is a firm of airplane manufacturers.

Compagnie française Thomson-Houston, despite its name, is a French company, established in 1893 to exploit the patents of two American engineers, which produces electrical and electronic equipment of all types.

Compagnie des Machines Bull S.A., a manufacturer of electrical and electronic machinery, was the main purely French producer of large and medium sized calculators. Bull sold out to the General Electric Company of America in 1964. The main reason for the sell-out was shortage of capital.

domains of knowledge, new chances for the domination of man over nature—destroyed by the barbaric commands of financial profit. The inert demands of capital come to oppose the living requirements of a creative praxis; to men who gave—and want to give—all of their creative capacities to a task which was their life and the meaning of their life, a task which made them part of a universal pursuit, capital suddenly says: "Stop; what you are doing doesn't pay and is therefore worthless. I pay you, so I tell you what to do. I owe you nothing because I paid you your salary. From now on you will mass produce components designed in Minnesota."

And technicians, engineers, students, researchers discover that they are wage earners like the others, paid for a piece of work which is "good" only to the degree that it is profitable in the short run. They discover that long-range research, creative work on original problems, and the love of workmanship are incompatible with the criteria of capitalist profitability—and this not because they lack economic profitability in the long run, but because there is less risk and more profit in manufacturing saucepans. They discover that they are ruled by the law of capital not only in their work but in all spheres of their life, because those who hold power over big industry also hold power over the State, the society, the region, the city, the university—over each individual's future.[4]

A contradiction breaks out between the power, the responsibility, and the mastery of the worker in productive praxis, and his powerlessness and servitude in relation to capital. He discovers that he is alienated not only as a worker but also as a citizen of Grenoble or of Saint-Nazaire, as a voter, as an individual on whom capital imposes from afar and from outside a future contrary to his plans, a prefabricated fate which will govern his life and that of his children and his fellow citizens.

It then becomes immediately evident that the struggle for a meaningful life is the struggle against the power of capital, and that this struggle must proceed without a break in continuity from

[4] See Pierre Belleville, *Une Nouvelle Classe Ouvrière* (Julliard, 1963), Chapter V.

the company level to the whole social sphere, from the union level to the political realm, from technology to culture. It is then up to the socialist movement to seize the baton and to carry the fight to its proper ground: the struggle for power. From then on everything is involved: jobs, wages, careers, the city, the regions, science, culture, and the possibility of developing individual creative abilities in the service of humanity. None of these things can be preserved or regained unless the power of decision passes out of the hands of capital into those of the workers. This goal will not be reached merely through nationalization (which risks turning into no more than bureaucratic governmentalization) of the centers of accumulation of capital and credit: it also requires the multiplication of centers of democratic decision making and their autonomy; that is to say, a complex and coordinated network of regional and local autonomous bodies. This demand, far from being abstract, has or can have all the urgency of imperious necessity. And this is true not only because unless this demand is satisfied entire regions with their present or potential wealth will die out, their inhabitants condemned to emigration, to diaspora, to the loss of their place in the world, their life, their mastery over their fate; this is true also because once a certain level of culture has been reached, the need for autonomy, the need to develop one's abilities freely and to give a purpose to one's life is experienced with the same intensity as an unsatisfied physiological necessity.

The impossibility of living which appeared to the proletarians of the last century as the impossibility of reproducing their labor power becomes for the workers of scientific or cultural industries the impossibility of putting their creative abilities to work. Industry in the last century took from the countryside men who were muscles, lungs, stomach: their muscles missed the open spaces, their lungs the fresh air, their stomachs fresh food; their health declined, and the acuteness of their need was but the empty functioning of their organs in a hostile surrounding world.[5] The industry of the second half of the twentieth century increasingly tends to take men from the universities and colleges, men who

[5] See J. P. Sartre, *Critique de la Raison Dialectique* (Paris: Gallimard, 1960), pp. 166 f.

have been able to acquire the ability to do creative or independent work; who have curiosity, the ability to synthesize, to analyze, to invent, and to assimilate, an ability which spins in a vacuum and runs the risk of perishing for lack of an opportunity to be usefully put to work.

In extreme cases, which are less rare than one might think, the need for autonomous activity, for creation and communication, assumes the acuteness of sharp pain. That is the case, for example, of the technicians in the nuclear industries, in Marcoule or elsewhere, who have a complete understanding of the functioning of the factory, who are able to intervene at any point in the system at the first sign of trouble, but who spend months, eight hours a day, sitting in front of screens which show them that the whole apparatus is working well, and therefore that they, with their intelligence and ability to intervene, are useless. Their boredom reaches the point of despair and neurosis. Powerless witnesses of a universe made by men but which makes men superfluous, they finally come to feel that they have to prove to themselves that they still exist, that they still have the ability to *do* something: at home, they take apart and put back together the most complicated apparatus (radio and television sets) on which to exercise their skills. At the end of several months, a few years at the most, they desert their "work" in order to escape breaking down or becoming insane.

This example is extreme, but significant and prophetic. Pottering around the house, keeping a garden or going fishing can save semi-skilled or unskilled laborers from a breakdown; but these avocations can no longer fill the vacuum created in the life of highly qualified but extremely specialized workers by the permanent underemployment of their abilities in passive and monotonous work. This example is indicative for the entire automated industry of the coming decade in which, as Marx foresaw, "human labor is reduced to a pure abstraction," [6] an empty activity, mere supervision.

But what this example also reveals is the extreme human and

[6] *Grundrisse*, pp. 695–6.

cultural misery to which not only the industry of advanced capitalism but above all its institutions, its education and its culture, have reduced the technical worker. This education, in its efforts to adapt the worker to his task in the shortest possible time, has given him the capacity for a minimum of independent activity. Out of fear of creating men who by virtue of the too "rich" development of their abilities would refuse to submit to the discipline of a too narrow task and to the industrial hierarchy, the effort has been made to stunt them from the beginning: they were designed to be competent but limited, active but docile, intelligent but ignorant of anything outside of their function, incapable of having a horizon beyond that of their task. In short, they were designed to be specialists. Anything in their education or even in their environment that could allow them to find outside their work the self-accomplishment denied them in their work has been eliminated. Any organs of power and of local self-determination which might permit the workers to shape if not their work at least their civic and cultural life have been eradicated from existing institutions. But for all that, the revolt of these new proletarians could not be prevented, even if the revolt still takes the silent form of powerless neurosis and of escape among these stunted and cheated men. Their successors, their younger colleagues, will understand the lesson of this disaster: they will refuse from the beginning to become stunted men.

It is in education that industrial capitalism will provoke the revolts which it attempts to avoid in its factories. Its maneuvers are too clear: in order to be able to produce its zombies without trouble, it has to be able to count on a mass of individuals whose horizons have been limited from early childhood. It needs a dualist education, like that which still prevails, for good reason, in Great Britain as the survival of the aristocratic power: the elite there has its "humanist" schools and education, and the people have others where utilitarian knowledge is disseminated. The choice is made according to birth and to wealth, beginning with primary school.

This system, however, is dying out, because it is unacceptable even in a merely formal democracy, but also because the British economy itself risks ruin as a result of it. Still, the Gaullist regime is trying to introduce it: it wants to introduce earlier specialization, to "industrialize the university," [7] to give quicker diplomas. It wants, in sum, to repeat on the educational level what in the sphere of leisure has been called "mass culture": the distribution of predigested parcels of knowledge—a cut-rate culture—by means of quicker courses followed by a practical apprenticeship. Instead of making clear the creative praxis which was at the origin of what has become *knowledge*, instead of giving the student the *means* of mastering comprehensively an area of knowledge and of locating this area with its interplay and relationship to other areas, instead of striving toward self-teaching and autonomous work in assimilation and research, what is being done is to make the student memorize out of context the ready-made results of the praxis of the past; the student is taught recipes and gimmicks to be mechanically applied to empirical problems. The student is made to ingurgitate a few chosen pages of knowledge; out of depths of carefully maintained ignorance a few little islands of knowledge will be permitted to emerge; "passivity and submission" [8] will be taught: the student will know enough to know how much he does not know, and to revere the science and the culture of the elite.

Now, this enterprise is a tissue of explosive contradictions, for to attempt to teach ignorance at the same time as knowledge, dependence at the same time as intellectual autonomy within narrow limits, is to expose oneself—if one cannot enforce a rigorous segregation—to the risk of seeing these limits and this ignorance challenged. "In order to be accepted," Simone Weil wrote, "slavery must last long enough every day to break something in a man." The remark is valid for the new proletarians of culture. If one cannot mutilate and specialize them from childhood, one cannot prevent them from feeling that the specialization and ignorance imposed on them, and the chances of autonomy and culture denied

[7] The expression is that of [education] minister Fouchet. Cf. Marc Kravetz, "Naissance d'un syndicalisme étudiant," *Les Temps Modernes*, February 1964.

[8] Marc Kravetz, *loc. cit.*

them, represent an inacceptable spoliation. There lies the possibility and the necessity for a cultural battle waged on all fronts by the socialist forces; against the subordination of education to ephemeral industrial requirements, and for the self-determination of education by the educators and the educated; against the academic mandarinate and utilitarian mass culture, and for an all-sided and integral education which permits individuals to measure the whole wealth of possibilities, to orient themselves according to their own needs and to orient society likewise.

Far from going contrary to technological evolution, this battle favors it. For it is not true that the technology of the present and of the future requires specialists; the only thing that is true is that the corporation heads demand specialists, and that is true for two reasons: because education, a so-called unproductive and unprofitable expense, lags qualitatively and above all quantitatively behind the requirements of the productive apparatus, and capitalist society is trying to catch up at the least cost, by cut-rate education; and because technically specialized manpower is more docile and adaptable to the increased intensity of industrial work.

These two political-economic reasons in fact run counter to the current of technology itself. In a state of constant upheaval, technology renders overly narrow specializations obsolete several times in each generation. Technology requires at the outset an all-sidedness, a solid theoretical foundation, in order to facilitate reconversions, reorientation, the continuous assimilation in the course of a productive life of new scientific and technical developments. In other words, if only from the professional viewpoint, the simple reproduction of labor power in its cultural components is no longer sufficient. The inculcation of a constant quantity of knowledge whose development during the course of productive life is not foreseen, sterilizes labor power at the outset: the worker's ability to create, adapt, and develop is too rigidly limited by his theoretical equipment. The rigidities which have been built into him either act as obstacles to more rapid development, or when this development does take place it passes him by and results in his disqualification, the premature depreciation of his educational capital, and ultimately in his unemployment.

The wider reproduction of labor power is therefore an objective necessity: professional ability can not be maintained today unless it grows; that is, unless there is continual accumulation of new abilities. The "labor bottlenecks" of which nearly all capitalist economies complain reflect in fact no more than the reluctance of capitalism to meet the social cost of this wider reproduction, to incorporate it into the cost of labor power itself. And this reluctance is logical: to consider the renewal and extension of the workers' abilities as an integral part of work would be to recognize that the worker works even when he is not producing merchandise, that he produces wealth even when he produces nothing that his employer can sell—nothing but the moral and intellectual resources which make up the worker himself as he makes himself in his work, that is to say when he is not unmade by the work others force upon him.

To agree to the wider reproduction of labor power would therefore be to agree that free time is not time lost doing nothing, but socially productive time in which the individual renews himself. At the same time it would be to admit that this labor power, produced and enlarged by the autonomous labor of the worker himself, has no other owner than the worker who produced it. It would, finally, be to admit that labor power is no longer merchandise to be used as one wishes once one has paid its market price, but that it *is* the worker himself, that it belongs to him by right, and that he has the right to determine its social use.

The workers' right to determine its social use means their right to control all possible and foreseeable modifications of the conditions under which their work is performed. It also means their right to exercise this control not only in order to subordinate these modifications to their need for human self-development, not only in order to guarantee that no one will extort from them a quantity or a quality of extra work, but also to make certain that they will be given the time and the means to expand their professional ability in conditions under their control, in view of foreseeable technological progress.

The wider reproduction of labor power is in itself socially productive work. As precondition and consequence of the increased range of social production, the acquisition of new qualifications is not to be made dependent on the solvency of each individual. Everything which concerns the professional education of workers is to be placed under the control of the workers themselves. All the time necessary for their education is to be considered as socially productive time, as societal work, to be paid accordingly. And that also holds true, obviously, for basic education. Individuals have the right to more than collective educational facilities. They also have the right to the constant and general elevation of their level of knowledge to the degree that social praxis becomes diversified and enriched. They have the right to a longer education and the right to co-determine their educational program themselves in conformity to their needs. And because this formative time is socially necessary as an initial precondition of social praxis its cost is not to be left to families: the provision of free education is also a fundamental demand.

2. *Creative Needs: Their Rise and Repression*

We again encounter here one of the profound contradictions of advanced capitalism: because of its essentially quantitative criteria it is unable to evaluate a development which tends more and more to become qualitative. It is, if one prefers, the contradiction between economic value and human purposes; and the latter cannot be grasped by the former because they are its foundation.

It is not only work itself which can no longer be evaluated economically because it is no longer a quantity of time and energy, a unitary merchandise, but a conscious exercise by qualified workers of their autonomy which carries in it as an activity of creation and of initiative its own sovereign requirements. It is also *labor power* which tends to escape quantitative evaluation: for qualified workers are no longer (and will become less and less) interchangeable vessels of physical energy whose power is worth nothing until and insofar as it is utilized and alienated by its purchaser, who combines it externally with other passive forces. No; the skilled workers of the leading industries, in the minority today but the majority of tomorrow, possess *in their own right*, unlike the classic proletarians, the labor power they lend. They possess it in their own right because they themselves acquired it, because they are in the best position to know how it should be utilized, because this power should not, can not even be combined externally with other powers, because from the beginning it has value only by virtue of its own ability to organize its relationships with the forces of others.[9]

It is truly impossible to order around the skilled worker of the pioneer industries;[10] he is at the same time both labor power and the owner of labor power; he is a *praxis subject* cooperating with other praxes in a common endeavor which could only be disorganized by too imperative directives from above. The worker, here, is an integral part of his labor power; it is no longer possible to quantify the latter by dissociating it from the former; one and the other share the same human autonomy.

From this derives a permanent conflict, whether latent or manifest, between scientific or technical workers, who are practically masters of their praxis, and the last surviving hierarchical subordination: the subordination of these workers to the possessive capital of the enterprise.

This conflict no longer essentially concerns the work situation, nor the exploitation of work, which is often highly paid. It hinges essentially on the contradiction between a sovereign praxis, which is an end unto itself, and an external, inert purpose, namely the requirement of capitalism to make praxis serve ends which negate it. Alienation within work tends to disappear—the teams of cultural and scientific workers are the only masters in their work—but the alienation of work continues, and tends to become intolerable, because of the limits and of the ultimate aim which the criteria of profitability (or of general policy, where public enterprises are concerned) impose on sovereign praxis.

[9] From which results, in practice, the fading away of hierarchical relationships in favor of team work. Cf. P. Belleville, *op cit.*, and S. Mallet, *La Nouvelle Classe Ouvrière* (Éditions du Seuil, 1963), especially the chapter on Caltex and the Introduction.

[10] E.g., nuclear, chemical, petro-chemical, energy, scientific, engineering, heavy construction, as well as the supervisory workers in automated factories, etc.

The limits of tolerability can be stretched for a long time by a managerial policy of "human relations" which respects the formal sovereignty of the worker, which tends to associate him with and to integrate him into the projects of capital. But this limit cannot be stretched indefinitely. The contradiction may erupt when the concern for immediate profitability prevents the workers from pursuing a project whose social fruitfulness and usefulness is clear to them (the cases of Neyrpic, SNECMA, Bull, Nord-Aviation, etc.). It may also erupt when a praxis which is in itself creative, and is conscious of itself as such, is utilized for purposes which represent its radical negation. In both cases the contempt of capitalism for creative praxis becomes evident, and the emancipation from the tyranny of capital becomes a fundamental demand.

In practice this is what happens in the capitalist countries every time and everywhere civilian research suffers for lack of sufficient funds while far superior resources are put at the disposition of military work. In all the capitalist countries science progresses only on the fringe and against the logic of capital because of military and prestige considerations, financed by government grants (which represent 80% of professional electronic activity and even more in the nuclear industry, more than half in aviation, and so on).

For scientific workers, this situation has a sinister irony: they cannot exercise their creative praxis unless they bow to the tyranny of capital, but they cannot bow to capital unless they put their creative activity in the service of bloodshed. They are burdened with a curse: either they do not exercise their praxis at all, or they exercise it against its grain. And this curse is comprehensive: it arises out of the logic as well as the power of capital.

Capital supports research only insofar as it is financially profitable. But long-term research (basic and theoretical) is never certain to yield returns; above all, the length of time required to make it pay is not calculable in advance. From the capitalist viewpoint, therefore, research does not pay well enough, not only because it is too great a risk in relation to the profit to be expected from it, but also, and above all, because *bigger* immediate profits can be made in real estate speculation, commerce, the entertainment industry, or in routine technical improvements.

Only governmental financing can therefore make research sufficiently economical. But capital, as political power and ideology, does not in general permit public financing except when public financing deducted in advance, as we have seen, partly from surplus and partly from the buying power of individual consumers, procures for the trusts profits which are as great or greater in a given situation than production for private demand. And the only way to arrive at this result is to make the State finance production which cannot be sold to the public, but which will be sold to the State itself at monopoly prices: military production.[11]

The fact is that biochemistry, genetics, medicine, etc., are progressing at a miserable pace, very much behind human potential; theory lags increasingly behind practice; and, unable to lay the foundations (by philosophical anthropology, and the philosophy of the sciences) of their own advances, the sciences and their techniques have ceased to be able to understand themselves—are in fact incapable of accounting for themselves.[12] Under a

[11] The Keynesian objection which holds that the State could procure for the monopolies equivalent profits by granting funds to finance socially useful research and production may be economically correct in certain sectors, but it neglects the political obstacles. To be exact:

1. It is economically correct only in the measure to which civilian research, publicly financed, rapidly results in civilian mass production; which is not the case for the electronic and nuclear sectors, for example. In the absence of military contracts, these industries would have no guarantee of a large market, with large profits, for their scientific products.

2. Governmental financing of large-scale civilian public interest projects presupposes the democratic determination of needs and their social satisfaction by means of a social redistribution of resources. But that would mean the end of the political power of capital, of its sway over production, and it would imply the redistribution of national income. The market economy would be undermined, public initiative would tend to replace private initiative, production and accumulation would fall under social control. (See the articles by Joseph Gillman, *Les Temps Modernes*, Nos. 188 and 189.)

[12] See E. Husserl, *Die Krisis der Europäischen Wissenschaften und die transzendentale Phänomenologie*, Gesammelte Werke, Vol. VI, Haag 1954.

capitalist regime, the reduction of military expenditures has never yet been coordinated with and accomplished for the benefit of increased social facilities and civilian research.

Militarization of science, industrialization of the university, commercial pollution of culture, subordination of the creation of human beings to the production of profits: we encounter the inability of capitalism (and, more generally, of political economy) to guarantee production geared to needs, to promote an expansion which is no longer quantitative but qualitative.[13]

The internal logic of the capitalist system identifies production as the production of salable goods or services and cannot measure wealth except in monetary terms. However, the world is not only

[13] Cf. J. K. Galbraith, "Economics and Aesthetics," *New York Herald Tribune*, January 17, 1964:

"Privately produced goods and services, even of the most frivolous sort, enjoy a moral sanction not accorded to any public services except defense. In fact, increasing private production . . . provides what we least need at the expense of what we most need. . . .

"We have developed an economic system of great power. We have good reason to be grateful for its achievements. But it naturally applies its power to its own objectives. It would be surprising were it not to use this power to bend people to its purposes. And if economic goals are preoccupying . . . we will accept the subordination of the individual, and therewith of the quality of life, to what seem to be economic imperatives. . . .

"The tobacco industry has not concealed its discontent with scientists who, on the basis of impeccable evidence, aver that cigarettes are a cause of lung cancer. The well-being of the industry requires the active and energetic recruitment of new customers at a reasonably early age . . . unhampered by adverse public propaganda. . . .

"The priority accorded to economic goals comes to focus in a conflict with truth and aesthetics. . . . The pre-eminence of economic values leads to the systematic appeal to a dream world which the mature, scientific reality would reject. . . . There is no necessary harmony between aesthetic and economic goals. One should assume a conflict. We have long accepted ugliness and squalor as the price of industrial progress. There is no reason why we should continue to do so. The social planning and expenditure which erases or limits grime and squalor and which preserves or restores beauty, which insures that art and culture are for their own sakes and not a byproduct of commercialism, will be costly. Some price in industrial efficiency should be assumed. . . .

"Economic achievement is an important part of life; it is not all."

produced in factories, nor is the increase of wealth measurable by the standards of increased surplus value. One and the other are produced wherever man shapes the world for man's sake, where he enters into relation with others and thus produces himself as a human being.[14]

This circumstance could remain hidden so long as the subordination of human requirements to the imperatives of production was made necessary by scarcity, as a precondition of survival: praxis then was no more than the means of producing necessities, and it saw itself as being inessential by comparison with the products which it served to tear out of nature's grip.

But we have seen that this relationship of subordination tends to become reversed due to a twofold process: the satisfaction of the most fundamental needs, and the improvement of productive techniques. At the same time as the individual becomes relatively emancipated from the pressure of vital needs (which would be in itself insufficient), he tends, because of the nature of his work, to understand himself as creative praxis which contains its own sovereign purposefulness. In the teamwork of highly skilled and equal workers who organize themselves in order to fulfill a task which no one else can tell them how to do, this praxis subject is no longer subordinate (inessential) by comparison to its object; it is rather a sovereign, self-determining activity for an object which reflects the group's liberty and confirms it. Work is therefore understood immediately as being not only the production of a predetermined *thing*, but as being first of all the production of a *relationship* between the workers. And the latter, because of the social and even international division of labor, are in communication (infinitely indirect, but nevertheless perceptible) with the entire world.

[14] "What is called work today is nothing more than . . . that repugnant and dangerous part of production which religion and morality honor with the name *work* and about which they have the audacity of spouting all sorts of phrases in the guise of benediction. . . . The morality of the world we live in takes care not to call work the free and pleasurable relationships among human beings." Marx, *The German Ideology*, "St. Max." [Translated from the German by Martin A. Nicolaus.]

Work is no longer only the production of merchandise objects; labor power is no longer subject only to the inertia of things; the worker is no longer only the instrument of a society attempting to organize its survival. Work, labor power, and worker tend to unite in the persons who produce themselves while producing a world. And this production takes place not only in the work situation but just as much in the schools, cafés, athletic fields; on voyages; in theatres, concerts, newspapers, books, expositions; in towns, neighborhoods, discussion and action groups—in short, wherever individuals enter into relationships with one another and produce the universe of human relationships.

More and more, this production tends to be an integral part not only of the production of man but of the necessarily wider reproduction of labor power itself. The international and intercontinental development of trade, the division of labor on an ever larger economic scale, the tendency toward regional and national specialization, the rapidity of communications, place every productive activity through the interplay of ever more numerous intermediaries into relationship with the entire world, and tend in practice to unify it.

It is impossible to produce artichokes in the León region or citrus fruits in Sicily without taking into account the activities of other producers, not only in León and Sicily, but in the French Midi, in Spain, and in Algeria. It is impossible to produce turbines in Grenoble without knowing what is being done in Milan, Ljubliana, in the Ruhr, and in Scotland. And this knowledge is part of the "labor power" not only of the commercial director or of the president of a cooperative, but also of every engineer, technician, supervisor, and, through the mediation of the latter, of every worker and every member of the cooperative. It is impossible in a modern production unit, even of medium size, to be on top of one's job without becoming familiar with world history in the process. And it is impossible to be ignorant of political, scientific, technical, socio-economic, and cultural evolution in the largest sense, or else one will lose the ability to enter into relationships with others, however close, or of suffering that absolute oppression which consists of knowing that one does not know what others know.

That is why cultural activity is an integral part of the necessarily broad reproduction of labor power, that is, of the ability of individuals to cooperate in a given common task. That also is why cultural activity is a *need*. And that, finally, is why the reduction of the "work" week remains a fundamental demand, together with the multiplication of cultural facilities and their self-management by the workers. The time necessary for the reproduction of labor power is not the same in 1964 as it was in 1904, for any kind of worker; just as it has never been the same for a concert pianist and for a piano tuner. The increase in free time is not an increase in idle time, but an increase in the socially productive time which is objectively and subjectively necessary for the production of human individuals and a human world.

Confronted by this necessity, it is true, neo-capitalist civilization has set up a gigantic apparatus of repression: an apparatus in the service of mystification, the perpetuation of ignorance, the destruction of culture, the conditioning of reflexes, and the transformation of free time into passive, empty time devoted to sterile diversions which a gentle terror summons every individual to perform. The need for culture must be deflected by corrupting it even as far as the consciousness it has of itself; it must be demeaned by offering it trashy objects, and by greeting cultural creation and its agents with derision in the name of primitivism and mass ethics.

Mass culture, a by-product of commercial propaganda, has as implicit content a mass ethic: playing on, maintaining, and flattering ignorance, it encourages the ignorant to resent those who "know," persuades them that the latter despise them, and encourages or provokes their contempt. This abject demagogy, one of whose elements—contempt for "intellectuals" (a term which has become an insult not only in the U.S.) and for culture—can be found in all fascist movements, professes no respect for exceptional individuals except insofar as their superiority can be accounted for by what they *are*, not by what they *do:* athletes, beauty queens, princely personages. This is because the superiority of *being,* physical or hereditary, can be taken as a product of the nature—of the soil, the race, the people, the nation—from which all individuals derive, and can thus reflect to them a natural bond of community with the hero, their own vicarious aristocracy, their original identity, reproclaimed in chauvinism.

This demagogy of leveling and of the least common denominator begins as business and ends as politics: in order to sell newspapers, radio time, or advertising space, one begins by flattering superstition and lulling reason, by emphasizing myths rather than facts, sensational rather than significant things; one prefabricates individuality in order to sell some of it to individuals whose own individuality one has destroyed (and which one destroys further by this forced sale), and one ends up preferring *and selling,* with the same commercial techniques, the "personality" of a Leader, a Chief, a paternal Dictator possessed of magic powers.

This gentle totalitarianism of monopoly civilization is a consequence as much as a cause.[15] It is a cause insofar as the sales technique of "affluent" capitalism is a technique of manipulation and of domination which aims deliberately at the psychological implantation in public life of the power of production and commerce, and the destruction of the forces which challenge it. It is a cause also insofar as it aims to destroy the concrete and autonomous communication between individuals, and their human relationships; insofar as it aims to conceal from the agents of praxis that the universe which they produce is in truth and in fact their own product. But this mystification, obviously, is possible only because it proceeds on a field which already favors it: because the destruction of the universe of human relationships, the uprooting of culture, the specialization and mutilation of individuals are already in advanced stages. This process originated in the backwardness which the "spontaneous" priorities of monopoly expansion imposed on the cultural and practical levels.

The insufficiency and then the degradation and industrialization of education; the repression of autonomous cultural activity

[15] See Herbert Marcuse, *One-Dimensional Man* (Boston: Beacon Press, 1964). I regret that I could not until now take into account this book which is in many ways remarkable.

by the militarization of industrial labor; the lack of collective cultural facilities; the rationing of free time; the more or less deliberate dispersion of workers in different locations (that is, the impossibility for them of communicating or meeting together after work, the obligation of living where they do not work and working where they do not live)—all this tends to create individuals who are isolated and beaten down, powerless because of their dispersion and their ignorance of the mechanisms which were born from their collective labor.

And it is among these underdeveloped and "mutilated" individuals (deliberately mutilated insofar as this made their exploitation easier and as their human development was considered an "unproductive expense") that monopoly capitalism, in order to perpetuate its domination, continues to repress and deflect the need for culture, to exploit and to flatter the feeling of powerlessness and of ignorance.

This is a particularly odious aspect of the subordination of individuals to production. But we have already seen that this subordination tends to become an obstacle for production itself; and that insofar as the latter requires workers who have a comprehensive vision of the productive cycle, of socio-economic processes and of the production process itself, a contradiction arises between the industrialization of culture and the culture of the industrial societies.

3. *Technocracy*

From then on, a double movement begins. At the bottom, in the technologically most advanced industries—as well as in the professionally qualified sectors of the small and medium peasantry—the workers move toward self-management (cooperative and regional, in the peasants' case) of the means of production and of local and regional life, a management for which they have the necessary competence. *Technological* power has already slipped away from the bourgeoisie (the owners) on this level, and their economic power is compromised by an inevitable process of financial concentration.

At the summit during this time the bourgeoisie sees its power limited by technocrats, specialists in coordination, planning and synthesis, tasks which the local economic agents, no matter how powerful they may be, are not able to perform. A narrow stratum of specialists is thus given sole responsibility for the task of centralizing and synthesizing—indispensable to the functioning of the overall system—a task for which the economic agents, whoever they may be, generally have neither the time, nor the competence, nor the information necessary. Totalitarian and dictatorial in the large sense, the technocratic apparatus has become the answer to a real necessity mainly *because of* a cultural Malthusianism which deprives individuals (including the majority of the bourgeoisie itself) of the competence necessary for self-management and democracy on all levels.[16] The decadence of political democracy, which technocracy likes to attribute to the senility of the parties and to the backwardness of political ideologies relative to economic realities, has therefore in fact some deeper reasons: it derives from the incapacity—which is in turn due to cultural and educational backwardness—of individuals, organized or not (the owners, political "elites," the bourgeoisie as a class, organized workers), to perform for themselves the management of social production and of society, on whatever level—local, regional, national; the industrial branch, the sector, the city.

Technocratic power, therefore, arises much less as a new form of the direct domination of monopoly capital and more as a contradictory and mediated form of this power. While its mem-

[16] The necessity for technocratic dictatorship (or centralization of real power) does not arise, in my opinion, from the need for central coordination and direction of decision making centers. The Yugoslavian system of self-management, which found itself, as was to be expected, faced with the problem of coordinating and integrating decentralized management units, has undertaken a solution which does not reinforce the central power: the 1963 Yugoslavian constitution assigns the task of coordination to specialized federal Assemblies made up of the representatives of self-management bodies of the various sectors (industries, culture and education, health, administration). The technocrats of the national Plan are controlled by these specialized Assemblies, by the federal Parliament, and by a Senate; and the right of self-management of all enterprises (including schools, hospitals, administration, etc.) is reinforced.

bers are most often of bourgeois origin, technocracy is not generally the errand boy of the monopolies and does not necessarily wield power as their representative. It is rather the mediator between the particular and contradictory interests of the capitalists on the one hand, the general interest of capitalism on the other, and finally the general interest of society.

The power of the technocracy cannot simply be identified with the direct, totalitarian power of monopoly capital, even though it also is a totalitarian power and even though this power is exercised *in fact* for the benefit of monopoly capital. Technocrats are much more than the trustees or the representatives of the power of the bourgeoisie as a class; they are rather a "caste": because they alone are specialized in the tasks of coordination and synthesis, they cannot accomplish these tasks without having—and without demanding, by virtue of their work, as an inherent requirement of their work—autonomy with regard to all interests, including the various interests of capitalist groups.

By its very function, technocracy tends therefore to locate itself "above the classes," to deny the necessity for class struggle, to set itself up as mediator and referee and in so doing to enter into contradiction with the classes. The famous "depoliticization" of the masses which technocracy pretends to take note of is not a fact it observes; it is rather the end it pursues, the result it wants to obtain—and does obtain in a very limited degree. *"Depoliticization" is the ideology of technocracy itself.* The so-called "neutrality" of the State is the ideology which justifies the power and the domination which technocracy is led to claim for itself by the logic of its situation.

The conflict of technocracy with the working classes as well as with the bourgeoisie is always profoundly ambiguous: this caste refuses from the outset to make decisions on the political terrain. Objectively progressive (or "on the left") in its conflicts with the monopolies, technocracy is subjectively conservative ("on the right") in its conflicts with the working class. Attempting to eliminate in advance the question of power, which it thinks can be held only by professional managers, it tries to keep a clear conscience in the midst of the contradictory criticisms to which it is exposed. Toward the monopolies it internalizes the conservatism of which the left accuses it by showing that the rationalization measures which it proposes consolidate and protect the capitalist system. Toward the labor movement it boasts of its conflicts with the monopolies in order to underscore its objectively progressive role.

This double game is obviously a mystification: to pretend to keep a balance between a bourgeoisie which is in power and a working class which is not is necessarily to play into the hands of the former. Technocracy is conservative ideologically (subjectively) to the very degree that its objective progressivism serves it as an alibi in its efforts to consolidate the existing system, to arbitrate its conflicts, and to absorb the anti-capitalist forces.

It shares this conservatism with all technicians insofar as they are empiricists. Conductor of an apparatus which interests him only for its smooth and efficient functioning, the technician cares a great deal more for the instrument than for the ends it serves. He lives from the beginning in a ready-made rationality with predetermined purposes which his work and his education do not lead him to question. The only truth, for him, is smooth functioning; and he sees value only in immediately applicable propositions. The rest is utopia.

However, this attitude is essentially fragile. The role of arbitrator and of neutral manager above classes and parties, dedicated to a rationality which transcends them—this role which technocracy attributes to itself is tenable only on three conditions:

1. That there exist no alternative to the type of rationality of the existing society, or that this alternative never be made sufficiently explicit to appear as a requirement already on the way to fulfillment, to unmask the present system. For this system is a combination of choices which anticipate certain solutions, purposes, and a certain model of life to the detriment of other choices, other purposes, a different model whose superior rationality would burst apart the irrationality of the present rationality.

2. That the incompetence of the anti-capitalist forces be evident, that their inability to manage the economy and the State without catastrophe strike the eye. Only this incompetence, this

glaring inability and the absence of an anti-capitalist alternative which is sufficiently worked out and coherent, can justify and confirm technocracy in its "vocation" of serving capitalism.

3. That the labor movement, on the other hand, be strong enough to counterbalance the pressure exercised by monopoly capital on the State, that is to say, on technocracy itself. Only a strong labor movement can prevent technocracy from becoming the servant of monopoly capital, the manager of a society in bondage, the accomplice of the repressions and cultural devastations of a capitalism without counterbalance.[17]

To the degree to which the incompetence of the labor movement and the absence of a coherent anti-capitalist perspective are real, technocracy will thus deploy its forces with the aim of attracting into its camp and integrating into the institutions of the capitalist State all the labor organizations which are susceptible to such a maneuver without, however, destroying the labor movement as a "loyal" opposition (or "countervailing power") to the power of monopoly capital.

If, on the other hand, the labor movement does not retreat into a defensive position but instead begins vigorously to work out an anti-capitalist alternative with strategically scaled and economically coherent objectives, then it will destroy the ideology which justifies technocracy; it will force technocracy to choose between the monopolies and the working class movement, and will win over a more than negligible portion of this "caste" to its side. This will be the case not only because the socialist movement can no longer appear to the technocrats as a simple protest movement, capable of destroying the apparatus of production but not of managing it for other ends; but also because a minority among the technocrats work for monopoly capital not out of conviction but because they find no other outlet for their competence, because they believe that they can follow a policy of the "lesser evil" and because they see no real road to socialism.

These technocrats are in the same position as that vast sector of lower and middle class groups who "sympathize" with socialism

[17] Cf. Bruno Trentin, "Les doctrines néo-capitalistes et l'idéologie des forces dominantes," *Les Temps Modernes*, September-October 1962.

but are in practice skeptical. They will not make a choice until they can see intermediate objectives, that is, mediations, which will make them see socialism not as something beyond the present society, separated from it by an unbreachable wall, but like the real horizon of the internal exigencies of this society—as a horizon toward which the progression of realizable intermediate objectives indicates a practicable way. Only the possibility of such a way will force this vague mass of "sympathizers" to make a choice which in the recent past it has all too often been spared.

Besides, the cooperation of technocrats is indispensable to the labor movement for the specification (but not the definition) of certain strategic objectives, of an economically coherent anti-monopolist alternative.[18] The fact is that the labor movement, in order to take power and to manage the State, needs specialized managers. But this requirement must not in any way imply that the socialist State can or should maintain the dictatorial and totalitarian character of the capitalist State, nor that socialism can, likewise, preserve for technocracy the monopoly of management, coordination, and organization of social relationships.

4. *The Crisis of Capitalist Values*

The formation of a technocracy as instrument and agent of the totalitarian and repressive power of the State arises in all

[18] See Jean Dru in *L'Express*, 30 January 1964.

The definition of objectives cannot be carried out except by the labor movement itself because these objectives must make social *needs* explicit, needs whose satisfaction requires structural reforms, that is to say, a modification in the relationship of powers. Once these objectives are defined, the collaboration of technicians is essential for determining how they may be made economically coherent, how soon they may be implemented, and therefore, in a limited way, which of them has priority. For no matter how wide sweeping structural reforms may be, not everything can be done at once; some things must have precedence over others.

To demand all at the same time (as has happened to the French Communist Party) the defense of small farmers and of small shopkeepers, an increase in social and cultural investment, an increase in wages and in private consumption, the reduction of the work week, and price stability results in a "program" of glaring inconsistency, whatever the economic system may be.

advanced industrialized societies, whether capitalist or socialist, because it is impossible for organized workers to manage their production and exchange by themselves. But this impossibility is not inherent in the complexity of social production and exchange. This impossibility, as we have already emphasized, is provoked—and in certain respects deliberately created—by cultural underdevelopment, by the mutilation of individuals in their work and even in their professional education, by the over-exploitation of labor power, i.e., the deprivation of free time and of cultural facilities, and finally by the absence or the deliberate liquidation of institutions and organs of democratic control.

This formidable repression has been justified up to now in the name of efficiency, of the need for an ever more specialized division of labor, with the aim of a rapidly increasing productivity and production of wealth. But with the advent of automation, this rationalizing and specializing tendency now reaches its limit: it must be reversed if advanced industrial civilization is to be something other than a barbaric system of waste and stupefaction. On the level of production itself, this tendency collides with a technological evolution which tends to reestablish the value of the many-sided worker and of autonomous praxis. The replacement of laborers and of semi-skilled workers who are tied down to their solitary work spot, by skilled teams who regulate their own cooperation themselves and who are conscious of their technical power and of their independence, creates a crisis within the hierarchy inside *and outside* the company.

The demand for self-management which arises out of productive praxis cannot be contained within the factory walls, the laboratories and research bureaus. Men who cannot be ordered around in their work cannot indefinitely be ordered around in their life as citizens, nor can they submit to the rigid decisions of central administrations.

The contemporary transition from mechanization to automation will bring about a crisis in the organization of work and the techniques of domination founded on it. The notion of individual output and even of labor time tends to fall by the wayside; the borderline between productive activity and leisure becomes confused; manual and intellectual work tend to go together and to cause the rebirth of a humanism of work which had been destroyed by Taylorism.[19] But this humanism of work is itself only a transitional form: automation will cause it in turn to disappear, as it destroyed it for the technicians of the nuclear plant at Marcoule, thus creating a crisis in the whole system of "values" of capitalist ideology. Already the latter denies the "values" of efficiency and of maximum output by proclaiming the "values" of affluent consumption and of comfort. "Its sweeping rationality, which propels efficiency and growth, is itself irrational. . . . Here, the social controls exact the overwhelming need for the production and consumption of waste; the need for stupefying work where it is no longer a real necessity; the need for modes of relaxation which soothe and prolong this stupefaction; the need for maintaining such deceptive liberties as free competition at administered prices, a free press which censors itself, free choice between brands and gadgets. . . . Advanced industrial society is approaching the stage where continued progress would demand the radical subversion of the prevailing direction and organization of progress." [20]

For capitalist civilization, efficiency, productivity, and output have always been the supreme "values"; these "values" now reveal themselves in their true light: as a religion of *means*. They could find their justification in the midst of acute scarcity by making possible an intense accumulation of the means of overcoming scarcity. In the midst of disappearing scarcity, they become a religion of waste and of factitious opulence. But these two value systems—the one which requires the worker to become subhuman in his work, and the one which requires him to consume superfluous goods—cannot long coexist. They could coexist only

[19] Frederick Winslow Taylor (1856–1915), an American engineer who was generally credited with pioneering the time-motion study of factory work. Taylor's method consisted of dividing each manual operation into a series of standard motion-components. He then eliminated "unessential" motions and so finally shaped the work process into the series of infinitely repeated simple tasks which are the essence of modern non-automated assembly-line manufacturing. [Translators' note.]

[20] Herbert Marcuse, *op. cit.*, pp. xiii, 7, 16.

if dehumanization in work were strong enough to make the workers unfit for any but sub-human and passive leisure and consumption. Such is no longer the case.

When an individual discovers himself as a praxis subject in his work it is no longer possible to make him consume and destroy superfluous wealth at the price of the essential element, his free disposal of himself. The creation of consumer wealth no longer needs to be bought at that price in the midst of disappearing scarcity. There is too glaring a disparity between the goods which "affluent" capitalism offers to individuals, and the possibilities which, in exchange, it denies to them by its pursuit of an ever greater efficiency, by the division of tasks and the centralization of power. "Thus, economic freedom would mean freedom *from* the economy—from being controlled by economic forces and relationships; freedom from the daily struggle for existence, from earning a living. Political freedom would mean liberation of the individuals *from* politics over which they have no effective control. Similarly, intellectual freedom would mean the restoration of individual thought now absorbed by mass communication and indoctrination, abolition of 'public opinion' together with its makers. The unrealistic sound of these propositions is indicative, not of their utopian character, but of the strength of the forces which prevent their realization." [21]

It also reveals the strength and the nature of the means that will have to be applied to break this opposition. The only humanism which can succeed the humanism of work is the humanism of free activity and of self-management at all levels. It presupposes that individuals instead of seeing themselves and being seen as means of society and of production, be seen and see themselves as ends, that no longer the time at work, but free time becomes the standard of wealth. As Marx wrote:

> But to the degree that big industry develops, the creation of real wealth comes to depend less on labor time and on the quantity of labor expended, and more on the power of the instruments brought into play . . . whose powerful effec-

[21] *Ibid.*, p. 4.

tiveness itself has no relation to the direct labor time necessary to produce them, but depends rather on the general level of science and the progress of technology, or on the application of this science to production. . . . Real wealth is manifest rather . . . in the monstrous disproportion between expended labor time and its product, and equally in the qualitative disproportion between work, reduced to a pure abstraction, and the power of the productive process which it supervises. Work appears less as a part of the productive process, for man relates to the productive process rather as supervisor and regulator. (*What is true for machinery also holds true for the combination of human activity and the development of human relationships* [emphasis added—A. G.].) It is no longer the worker who inserts a modified natural object [i.e., a tool—A. G.] between himself and the object; he rather inserts the process of nature, transformed by him into an industrial process, as a link between him and inorganic nature, whose master he becomes. He stands at the side of the productive process, instead of being its chief agent. In this transformation, the great fundamental pillar of production and of wealth is neither the direct labor which man performs, nor the time he works, but *the appropriation of his own productive force in general* [emphasis added—A. G.], his understanding of nature and his mastery over nature in his existence as a social being—in a word, the development of the social individual. . . . As soon as labor, in its direct form, has ceased to be the great source of wealth, labor time ceases and must cease to be its measure, and exchange value the measure of use value. The *surplus labor of the masses* has ceased to be the precondition of the development of collective wealth, and the *idleness of the few* for the development of the general powers of human thought. . . . The free development of individuals, and therefore not the reduction of necessary labor time to create surplus labor, but in general the reduction to a minimum of necessary labor time in the society [becomes the goal of production—A. G.], which then corresponds to the artistic, scientific, etc. development of individuals in the time which has become free and with the means that have been created for all. Capital is its own contradiction in this process, for it seeks to reduce labor time to

> a minimum, while at the same time postulating labor time as the sole measure and source of wealth. *It therefore reduces necessary labor time, in order to increase superfluous labor time; in an increasing measure, therefore, it posits superfluous labor time as the precondition—a question of life and death—of the necessary* [emphasis added—A. G.]. Thus, on the one hand, it enlists all the powers of science and nature, as well as of social organization and social intercourse, in order to make the creation of wealth (relatively) independent of labor time expended. On the other hand, it wants to measure the gigantic social forces created in this way by means of labor time, and to restrict these forces within the limits necessary to preserve already-created value as value. Productive power and social relationships—which are different sides of the development of the social individual—appear to capital only as means, and are only means to allow it to produce on its restricted base. But in fact these are the material preconditions to blow this base to pieces. . . .
>
> The measure of wealth is then not labor time at all, but disposable time.[22]

It is neither utopian nor premature to wage a struggle in this perspective. Automation will be a reality in the industrialized societies before the end of the century. At least one generation will be necessary to rid individuals of the idea that they are the tools of their tools, to accustom them to a liberty which will be within their reach, and of which the sociologists only demonstrate that it "is frightening," without demonstrating at the same time that this fright is due to the emptiness with which the dictatorship of efficiency and profit has filled the men it mutilates.

"The ultimate cause of the degradation of leisure is to be found in the degradation of *work* and of *society*";[23] in the subordination of the State to the interests of capital, in the destruction of the organs and institutions of democracy, bypassed by the fundamental decisions of those who wield power in the economy, free of control by elected assemblies. As the technicians who presently

[22] *Grundrisse*, pp. 592–594, 596. [Translated from the German by Martin A. Nicolaus.]

[23] Ernest Mandel, *Traité d'Economie Marxiste* (Julliard, ed.), II, p. 363.

die of boredom in Marcoule, Lacq, and elsewhere—administered with a very bureaucratic and distant efficiency by officials who are equally bored—become the predominant reality, the path of liberation will inevitably proceed through the individuals' conquest of the right to "administer" themselves in their work, their company, their community, their leisure, their home, their cultural and social services.

But when that day comes it may well be too late already if the preparations for this conquest are not begun now. The despecialization, generalization, and the autonomous management of higher education, the decommercialization of the media and of culture, the decentralization and multiplication of centers of democratic decision making, the enlargement of local, provincial, and regional autonomies, the multiplication of self-managed cultural centers and installations are all fundamental demands from now on.

5. *The Cultural Battle*

"To be sure," writes Herbert Marcuse, "labor must precede the reduction of labor, and industrialization must precede the development of human needs and satisfactions. But as all freedom depends on the conquest of alien necessity, the realization of freedom depends on the *techniques* of this conquest." [24] The means determine the end, and when the end is the "all-sided development of the individual," the means cannot be left to chance.

The de facto dictatorship of organized capitalism can no longer be combatted in the advanced industrial countries in the name of an opposed dictatorship or a dictatorship which differs only in details and color scheme. It is impossible to fight against it only on the economic and political fields. The dictatorship of capital is exercised not only on the production and distribution of wealth, but with equal force on the manner of producing, on the model of consumption, and on the manner of consuming, the manner of working, thinking, living. As much as over the workers, the factories, and the State, this dictatorship rules over the society's vision of the future, its ideology, its priorities and goals; over the

[24] *Op. cit.*, p. 18.

way in which people experience and learn about themselves, their potentials, their relations with other people and with the rest of the world. This dictatorship is economic, political, cultural, and psychological at the same time: it is total.

That is why it is right to fight it as a whole, on all levels, in the name of an overall alternative. A battle which is not from the beginning waged on the cultural, "ideological," and theoretical fields as well as on the *main* battleground, would be in vain—as vain as a battle fought in the name of an overall alternative but without knowing how to embody it in mediations, without knowing how to link it to immediate struggles and needs.

The cultural battle for a new conception of man, of life, education, work, and civilization, is the precondition for the success of all the other battles for socialism because it establishes their meaning. But the precondition for waging this battle is a labor movement which has abandoned its cult of conformity and all schematicism, which has reestablished research and theoretical creativity with full rights and autonomy, which lets all disputes develop freely, which does not subordinate theory to ephemeral tactical opportunities. Never has the workers' movement had so great a need of theorists, and never in France has it been so poor in them, abandoning immense fields of potentially creative research to empiricist sociologists, abandoning with the same blow to neo-capitalism the task of forging an ideology of consolidation and justification for the ever growing strata of non-manual workers.

If Marxism—as the humanism of praxis and of free human development—wanted to play a losing game, it would go about it no differently. In fact, it has everything to gain by occupying itself with all problems and by enriching itself, insofar as these problems have concrete substance, with the currents and researches which proceed in its margins.

"The deepening contradiction between monopolist development and the most profound human ideological and professional requirements of the intermediate social strata, cannot ripen except through the mediation of the elites, of the avant-garde which are capable of interpreting the deepest demands, the most permanent interests of these social groups. . . . The contents which the proletariat can directly express are not really sufficient to constitute a positive critique of the capitalist system. . . . Power will not be achieved by the proletariat without the lasting alliance of the social and political forces which can adhere to a revolutionary solution only insofar as they can see it as a well-defined positive whole. The ideals of Communist society, its content, its institutions, and values, can not therefore remain a vague promise for the future (if they ever could), but must become, even in the form of successive approximations, a decisive preliminary element of the struggle for power." [25]

The Western labor movement cannot wait for the positive model of the society that is to be constructed to be furnished to it from outside. Certainly one can speculate that automation will bring all the capitalist societies to the point of crisis; it will destroy the quantitative criteria of efficiency on which these societies are based; automation will make it clear that the rational utilization of machines (fixed capital) according to the exigencies of maximum profitability cannot be achieved except at the price of an irrational utilization of men, of their time and their abilities, to the detriment of their human exigencies. One may further speculate that automation will be imposed on the capitalist societies by the advanced socialist societies, for whom there are no economic and ideological obstacles (although there are bureaucratic ones) to its application.

But this kind of speculation would simply defer the problem a generation or more while permitting the continued existence of the risk that capitalism, in order to maintain its criteria of rationality, will defend itself against the social and political consequences of automation by the organization of waste and destruction on a global scale. It is not possible to wait until a ready-made model is furnished by the socialist societies, which are barely emerging from decades of forced accumulation. They are not very far advanced in the theoretical investigation of the purposes and the model of life. All investigations to that purpose in the "Western" socialist movement will be for them a positive contribution.

[25] Lucio Magri, *op. cit.*, pp. 616, 619.

PART TWO

The Labor Movement and the Common Market

Introduction

At the beginning of 1963, when the negotiations between Great Britain and the European Economic Community (EEC) had broken down, two governments of continental Europe considered putting an end to the experiment of European integration. A few hours of deliberation, however, made it clear that to do so would be impossible: even though the European Community was not yet a political reality, although the Community's policy had not progressed beyond the tentative initial stage of clearly restricted plans and projects—transportation, energy, agriculture—the European Economic Community had become an irreversible fact. A "European" economic space had been born even before its institutional framework could be set up, a space created by arrangements, agreements, interpenetration, and above all by the investment programs of trusts and other financial groups whose activity, five years after the Treaty of Rome had taken effect, covered most or all of the Common Market.

Thousands of mergers, stock barters, production and market agreements, cartelizations, creation of subsidiaries, have already covered the area of the EEC with a network of "plans," sometimes coordinated, often overlapping. These processes have resulted in the birth—on the level of holding, trust, and investment companies, of monopolistic interpenetration, and of "European" manufacturers' associations—of centers of decision making and centers which escape the control of the different national governments.

The full extent of the problem created for economic planning on the regional, national, or supranational levels by the internationalization of capital then became clear. A multiplicity of private "plans" were already in operation which restricted the national plans' freedom of action and imposed private decisions and orientations in matters of political economy on the governments of Europe.

The free circulation of capital, especially the concentration of American capital in a few sensitive industries, renders one of the weapons of governmental regulation ineffective: the selective orientation of credit and fiscal policy. Whether it liked it or not, for example, the French government had to tolerate the creation by Anglo-Saxon capital of enterprises whose dimensions made sense only on the level of the entire Common Market, and whose establishment sometimes ran counter to the French national plan's geographic, economic, and social priorities.

The "free play of prices" postulated by the liberal ideology of the Treaty of Rome, on the other hand, tolled the knell of a whole series of direct and indirect subsidies (decentralization incentives, tax relief, special freight rates) by means of which the State took upon itself a part of production costs in order to keep alive certain enterprises and regions which were incapable of surviving under competitive conditions.

However, in other respects the national economic plans (or what passes for plans) found themselves confronted by the incipient fusion of the different national economies, with tasks new in scope or in nature, which tended to enlarge, rather than to diminish the scope of public intervention.

These tasks principally include reorganization, professional and vocational training, city planning, regional development planning, and restructuring, in connection with the reconversion of traditional sectors of economic activity which are suddenly deprived of their protection and their subsidies, such as the extractive industries, shipbuilding, and agriculture.

The first five years of the Common Market have therefore brought contradictory results: in certain sectors the possibilities for public intervention are reduced and the centers of power tend to escape national control. This is the case notably in the basic industries, in the mass-consumption industry, and in transportation. In other areas, on the other hand—agricultural, regional, and wage policies notably—the governments find economic planning more necessary than ever. The governments are at least potentially exposed to the pressures of the working masses, because all-European considerations still exercise little or no influence on the orientation and content of public planning in these areas.

Can we conclude therefore that the Common Market has created in each national economy a series of new contradictions which offer new possibilities for the initiative of the socialist forces? And if the answer is affirmative, can these initiatives proceed on the level of economic planning? If so, on the national or on the supra-national level?

In order to locate these questions within their context, I will first outline the dominant features of the changes which the Common Market has brought about in private enterprise. I will then raise the question as to whether there is agreement or contradiction between these changes and the heightened necessity for national planning, which in its turn requires a more or less pronounced supranational planning. It goes without saying that this investigation can arrive at no fixed and final conclusions because the sharpness and the nature of the contradictions here examined depend in large measure on the degree of consciousness and militancy displayed by the organized working class.

CHAPTER ONE

Europe for the Monopolies

THE FIRST FOUR YEARS of the Common Market have seen a yearly average of about one thousand "mergers and agreements" between companies of different nationalities, and an approximately equal number of mergers and agreements between French firms.

French planners generally consider this a beneficial process. International competition and the fear of foreign competition have in fact been much more effective than mere persuasion in stimulating French industry (and to a lesser degree agriculture) to modernize its methods.

Without a doubt the Common Market is a consequence of monopolist expansion and not its principal cause. But it must also be understood that monopolist expansion needed the Common Market as a prerequisite of its continuation.

Technological evolution and the increase in the dimensions of productive units and of the volume of fixed capital brought about thereby required an extension of the market. Without this extension, the national oligopolies would have found it impossible profitably to introduce the potentials of modern technology and mass production. The national oligopolies would have fallen into a state of permanent inferiority to the American trusts, with all the consequences of such a development on the level of inter-imperialist rivalry.

At least in France, technocrats have followed this line of reasoning much more than businessmen. The opening of the national borders and the creation of a large economic space would put the national monopolies into competition with their foreign counterparts, destroy their comfortable routines, force them to develop technologically and increase in size. This result has in fact been largely achieved.

In the first phase, which is now drawing to its conclusion, the lowering of customs barriers has broken in each of the six countries of the EEC a good number of old arrangements based on tacit or hidden cartels agreements and on Malthusian monopolist practices.

The most general pattern was that of the coexistence of powerful, highly monopolized groups in the majority of industrial sectors, surrounded by a swarm of small and minute, often marginal, enterprises. The latter, serving as shock absorbers and buffers for the former, allowed the monopolies to set their prices according to that of the least economical among the enterprises, and thus to reap substantial super-profits due to their technological advantage. The existence of a great number of marginal enterprises also allowed the manufacturers' association in a given industrial branch to complain to the State of its numerous hardships in order to obtain fiscal advantages and protective tariffs from which the monopolies were the first to benefit.

The monopolies' super-profits were reinvested only to a limited degree; often the monopolies considered modern techniques too costly to be profitably introduced for the national market. The tariff protection which they enjoyed also allowed them to consider the adoption of these techniques—and serious research efforts—as superfluous luxuries, except in the sectors and the companies which depended heavily on the export trade.

The Common Market has disturbed these comfortable routines. It has made the domestic monopolies fear the competition of those of their foreign counterparts who are technically more advanced and often dispose of excess capacity. The opening of the national borders has destroyed or diminished the hold of the monopolies on the domestic market, and cartelization has tended to give way to monopolist competition. In other words, each domestic monopoly, fearing that foreign monopolies will invade its markets and capture a major corner of the Common Market, must save itself by rushing ahead. In order to maintain its position, each monopoly has to strengthen its productive and competitive ability in order to be able to compete with the foreign monopolies in the latter's interior markets. In case of success, the foreign adversaries will no doubt retreat in the face of a ruinous trial of strength, and will avoid being drawn into a price fight.

Approximately all of the monopolies of the EEC and of Great Britain have reasoned along this line. The resulting race of investment (and over-investment), of technological innovation, of modernization and rationalization has been *one* of the factors behind the European economic boom of the last five years.

However, like armies arranging their order of battle, the monopolies could not hold all the ground they had occupied at the outstart. The expansion of their overall activity was paralleled by tactical retreats in certain of their productions: it is better to abandon at the outset a line of products which foreign competitors are in a clearly superior position to sell, and to concentrate on positions which one has a good chance of holding and improving. A double movement of specialization has thus come about. First of all, on the national level, monopolies which were once considered competitors have merged their costly research, sales or production departments. Each company's range of products has tended to narrow due to specialization agreements, in order to achieve mass production and a lower unit cost. The most well known French examples of this process are the merger of Rhône-Poulenc and Celtex (artificial fibers) and the merger of the chemical departments of Péchiney and Saint-Gobain.

Parallel to the specialization agreements between domestic firms there have been a great number of international agreements: exchange and acquisition of patents and licenses (especially in the nuclear industries), sharing of technical and commercial services (for example, in the automobile industry, Fiat-NSU, Renault-Alfa Romeo), reciprocal stock acquisitions, alliances of two monopolies against a third, etc. But also, outside of this process and contradictory to it, many foreign trusts have bought out small or medium-sized domestic enterprises in order to get a direct foothold on the domestic market and to compete more effectively against the indigenous monopoly.

One of the first stated objectives of the Common Market has thus been partially achieved: no longer treated with gentle hands by the monopolies, the more or less marginal enterprises, precapitalist or family firms, have been largely eliminated. Notably, twenty per cent of the small electrical construction companies and thirty per cent of the small textile manufacturers in France have disappeared. There has been an almost universal stampede in the French food industry, where the individual companies (most of them artisan-style and family operated, but also the biscuit trusts, for example) were sold into American hands at the first opportunity in order to survive. Their survival, by the way, was nothing more than the occupational and financial "survival" of the owners who, by selling out and becoming wage earners, earn several times what the continuation of their former activity would have brought in.

A second objective of the Common Market is EEC-wide specialization, in conformity with the world-wide tendency toward the internationalization of production and the international division of labor. But it is precisely the manner in which this process of internationalization under conditions of monopolist competition is being carried out which gives rise to the necessity for a certain amount of planning.

According to the idyllic vision of the Common Market, the creation of an economic space comparable in size to that of the United States should create production units as powerful and as rational as the American ones throughout Europe. With the pressure of competition, prices should fall, the standard of living should rise, and an "American-style" prosperity should result.

In fact, as both Marxist and bourgeois economists had predicted, the monopolist expansion over the last few years has created three factors of imbalance and disturbance:

1. A false orientation of investment, and over-investment;
2. Unfavorable geographic distribution of investments;
3. The crisis in agriculture, which can be considered as one particular aspect of the preceding point, because it arises principally (but not uniquely) in areas where relatively little industrial investment occurs.

To what degree can the type of "planning" which is compatible with the capitalist system remedy these imbalances and distortions? What kind of "planning" do the EEC, its governments, and its dominant private groups find necessary? After having examined these questions, I will sketch a critique of this minimal "planning" and try to indicate what possibilities are open to the working class movement to work toward different orientations.

1. *Toward Cartelization*

In the absence of a natural complementarity among the various national economies, specialization and division of labor on the European scale cannot be considered as rational measures unless the international distribution of tasks is coordinated; unless, that is, the manufacturers' associations of the various industrial sectors were to exchange their views regularly, to communicate to each other their forecasts and plans, their investment programs, and unless in the framework of these meetings they worked toward general cartelization on the all-European scale: division of markets; division of products by quantity, quality, and nature; coordination of investments and of price policies.

This kind of cartelization is highly advanced in certain industries (light bulbs, radio and telephone components, pharmaceutical products, heavy machinery, etc.), where it began in the period between the two world wars. At the moment, however, cartels which cover all six countries of the EEC with one given product are still exceptional.[1] One of the first reasons for this, as we saw, is the breakup of the former domestic cartel agreements under the pressure of foreign competition. A second reason is the invasion of the Common Market by the American trusts which, although they are linked at home, in their domestic market, by cartel agreements which are often quite old, nevertheless take up the fight again on European territory in the hope of improving their position in the United States by increasing their strength abroad.

The competitive fight waged by the American trusts in Europe (where their investments have doubled in five years) in the hope of getting the lion's share of the only profitable market available for American consumer goods outside of the U.S., forces the

[1] The EEC Treaty Committee estimates the number of cartel agreements at about one thousand. Nevertheless, with the exception of the examples cited above, these agreements do not involve *all* of the principal European producers in a given industry.

European trusts in their turn to accelerate their expansion, sometimes by uniting against the invader but more often by speeding up their production.

In the automobile industry, for example, the disproportionate investments by Ford and General Motors (whose productive capacities have quintupled and tripled, respectively, in Germany in four years) at first provoked an investment race among the big European manufacturers, including the British. European productive capacity will, according to present manufacturers' programs, reach 8.5 million vehicles in 1965, for an internal and external market of at most 5.5 million vehicles. Therefore, unless the price structure crumbles, a 55 per cent overproduction will take place.

Likewise, in the synthetic fiber industry as in the tire, agricultural machinery, and petrochemical industries, the threshold of rationality has already been overstepped; huge excess capacities exist, and partial unemployment, the close-down of production units, and personnel cutbacks are frequent. For example, the isotactic polypropylene (a new plastic fiber) factory built by Montecatini[2] in Brindisi largely with public funds in order to compete against the three big American synthetic fiber trusts (DuPont, Monsanto, and American Cyanamid) will have no outlet for its capacity until four or five years from now. The same is true for the French Dunlop factories, which have been expanded in order to compete with the American trusts Firestone and Goodyear; and for the agricultural equipment plants which have been established or expanded in France in order to compete with Massey-Ferguson, John Deere, and International Harvester.

Thus, for the moment, the Common Market escapes cartelization only to fall into over-investment and the waste of resources which might be put to socially and economically beneficial uses. The immediate result has been an investment boom which has, however, been dying out since 1962.

[2] *Società Generale per l'Industria Mineraria e Chimica Anonima, Montecatini*, established in 1883, is today the largest Italian group in the mining and chemical industries. (Among its many subsidiaries is Monteshell Petrochimica S.p.A. Brindisi.)

It will be followed by a transitional phase whose beginnings can already be observed, namely a new thrust of industrial and especially financial concentration.[3] The latter will create the objective preconditions for a general cartelization in all industrial branches, a cartelization which may be secret and Malthusian but more probably will be overt and approved by the Executive Committee in Brussels.

In effect, for the past few decades the competition between trusts has ceased to take the form of price wars, which are ruinous for all participants, uncertain in outcome, risk provoking serious social troubles, and, in the case of the Common Market, risk provoking governmental intervention to bail out a capitalist trust in difficulties. In addition, as a director of I. G. Farben wrote before the war, "A price war benefits only the consumer, but the maintenance of a certain price level is to the advantage of all competitors." For more than thirty years the American automobile trusts have competed with each other only on the basis of minor innovations, always accompanied by approximately parallel price raises.

2. *Is "European Planning" Possible?*

Precisely because of their devastating power, the commercial weapons wielded by the trusts will never be used; these weapons will make price wars improbable, and will permit each group to enter into the inevitable negotiations (cartelizations) from a position of strength. However, the danger of accidents is always present, and one cannot exclude the possibility that the social cost of monopolist competition and the waste it entails will cause popular uprisings. In 1961 Mr. Claude Gruson voiced regret that "France was forced to develop a much stronger export potential than would have been necessary within the framework of a coordinated development policy." And he let it be understood that

[3] One of the major directors of the French automobile industry declared in the autumn of 1963 that Europe has room for only three big companies if the automobile industry wants to be able to stand up to the three big American corporations. He added that the financial concentration of the industry (on the model of the British BMC or the American General Motors) would not create a corresponding technical concentration.

private over-investment might be incompatible with the social objectives of the French "plan." Along with Mr. Gruson, the majority of European technocrats now favor a coordinated investment "program" on the EEC level, in other words, supranational "French-style planning," based on the confrontation of the public and private programs.

We will see below that such "planning," while it may eventually adjust investments to the development of market demand—instead of letting investments be used as a weapon of conquest—will nevertheless not adjust investments to real needs. But what is important at the moment is that such European programming as it is presently conceived would have the same effects in practice as a general cartelization (although it would be more rational), and without a doubt will not become a reality until the preconditions of the latter are ripe, that is, after a new phase of intense monopolist concentration.

European technocracy, by the way, is more or less aware of this fact, and its intention is to hasten the ripening of these preconditions, which are both objective and subjective. The struggle of the big private corporations, which in each country are supported or patronized by the State against their competitors abroad, is in effect so complex that as soon as an equilibrium is about to be established, the entrance of a new trust (often based outside the EEC), or a technological breakthrough, or a new product again modifies the relationship of forces and launches a new round of competition and over-investment. To the degree that the trusts themselves become aware of the financial risks of the competition in which they are engaged (as in the automobile, the heavy electrical and mechanical construction industries, etc.),[4] European technocracy will touch on a sensitive nerve and perhaps bring them to their senses with the proposal of European "planning."

This planning obviously has nothing in common with real economic planning. Following the French formula, this process con-

[4] In October 1963, Georges Héreil, President of Simca (which is controlled by Chrysler), publicly called for a "European Automobile Construction Community" to be responsible for "rationalizing" both European and American investments in this industry.

sists of bringing business representatives together in the same room in order to let them enlighten each other with general considerations about the business cycle, the prospective condition of the market, and the supply-demand-investment equilibrium, and in order to let them then discover, during the course of hopefully ever more frank discussions, whether or not their respective intentions, laid end to end, are economically coherent. If not, adjustments come about through mutual confrontation of the participants—through the "self-discipline" they impose on themselves, if any—rather than through the eventual directives of the "planners." The latter, therefore, essentially become catalysts of whatever adjustments and agreements are reached (and it takes a very subtle intelligence to distinguish them from cartelization), which they thereby endorse and whose profitability they underwrite. The capitalists' freedom of action remains untouched but their decisions are better informed, and the pursuit of maximum profit remains the ruling criterion. In the rare cases where the "planners" intervene directly, their actions lack the force of authority. Instead, their intervention consists of guaranteeing a profit, through tax exemptions, bonuses, and other financial inducements, for uneconomical operations; that is, to cover capitalist risks and guarantee capitalist profits.

The extension of "French-style planning" to the entire EEC is nevertheless not certain, although its partisans are gaining ground. The decisive battle for them will begin when the recession whose first signs were visible in 1963 reveals the full extent of the accumulated excess capacity. The recession will also expose the inability of the individual governments, having been deprived of their power of economic intervention by the Treaty of Rome, to guarantee capitalist profit and the social tolerability of the system, and it will make clear that it is necessary to have recourse to new forms of public regulation and initiative in order to insure profitable investment, the continuation of economic expansion, and a tolerable standard of living for the majority of the people.

The victory of the "planners," although likely at that moment, nevertheless will not be achieved without bitter conflicts, because it is possible to predict that the economic recession will produce three distinct pressures on European institutions:

1. "Liberal" pressures, which will tend to let a new equilibrium establish itself after a painful phase of readjustment;

2. Inverse pressures tending to stop the experiment, to dismantle "Europe," to give the individual governments the powers to carry out an autonomous, authoritarian, and protectionist economic policy in order to overcome the crisis;

3. Pressures, finally, to "save Europe," a Europe threatened by disintegration, by creating on the supranational level the instruments of intervention, stabilization, and planning which the individual governments have lost.

It is not difficult to imagine where these pressures will come from:

1. The first from the United States, for political as well as economic reasons (the commercial and technical domination of Europe by the United States within an "Atlantic market" being a guarantee of the political unity of the entire Atlantic community, as *inversely*, the political unity of the community is a guarantee that the United States will be able to continue to dominate its markets), with the support of an important part of the European banks, and of German, Dutch, and British big business.

2. The second from the pre-capitalist and paleo-capitalist strata (family businesses, small shopkeepers, small and medium peasantry), and perhaps from a part of the labor movement;

3. The third from European technocracy, from neo-capitalist big business, and from the Social Democrats.

Which of these three possible developments offers the greatest possibilities to the working class movement?

1. The first is to be rejected out of hand: it will bring about the literal and figurative "Americanization" of Europe. It would force the working classes to carry the entire burden of sectoral and regional readjustments and reorganization. Pitiless repression would accompany the social struggles provoked by massive layoffs and transfers; while at the same time the very unequal geographical distribution of the effects of the recession (a profound

crisis in one region or sector may go together with increased prosperity and higher wages in others, as during recent American recessions) would create unfavorable conditions for general national and international working class action.

2. The second development may seem to offer better possibilities. In its initial phase it would offer the possibility of a power seizure by a loose coalition of the pre-capitalist middle class and of the working class in one or two countries of the EEC, while the others (West Germany and Holland particularly) would tighten their bonds with the United States. In the countries which break with the EEC the return to protectionism and to national economic regulation would be incapable of creating outlets for the excess capacity accumulated by and for the Common Market. Only a medium-range program to reorganize the productive apparatus could reestablish full employment.

But such a program could be carried out only on public initiative, that is, by the nationalization of the principal centers of economic power. The mixed coalition formed to undo "Europe" would certainly break apart when the time came to define its economic policy. Its left wing would be forced to engage in an experiment with socialist power whose fruits could not appear for several years and which would be carried out under unfavorable economic conditions (a general flight of capital, a drying up of the principal sources of accumulation, boycott by other capitalist countries). Politically isolated internally, it would be forced to resort to repressive measures which would aggravate its external isolation. Can socialism be established under such conditions? It is not impossible. But it would be a case of "socialism in one country," a Western country, surrounded, vulnerable to the propaganda of its neighbors and exposed to their commercial blockade. This experiment, therefore, would have little chance of producing an attractive socialist model except in the very long run. If it failed to establish itself on a permanent footing, the first of the developments foreseen above would succeed it.

We must nevertheless not reject the second path out of hand. Its risks are enormous (the risk of failure, which would discredit socialism for a long time, the risk of deviation and of degeneration), but in a certain international situation they may not be prohibitive.[5] The risks are serious enough, however, to make it advisable for the labor and socialist movements not to stake everything on the breakup of the EEC and to prepare, in addition, an alternative strategy within the framework of the third possible development: the creation of a supranational European State.

3. The latter seems probable at present. To the degree that traditional democracy is everywhere decadent, short-circuited in all important decisions by a governmental technocracy which serves as mediator between the interests of big capital and the interests of society; to that degree is supranational regulation likely to be demanded by the different national bourgeoisies as the most rational solution, both from the viewpoint of capitalist economics and that of political stability. Within the EEC the capitalist groups which favor an "Atlantic market," that is to say, a neo-liberal economy with a minimum of public regulation, are a declining minority. Capitalist "planning" appears as a necessity in all the mature capitalist economies, not only in order to guarantee monopoly profits but equally to underwrite the social cost of "free enterprise" and to make the system socially tolerable. When the profits and the social tolerability of capitalism are undermined by the dismantling of governmental powers and by a recession, as will inevitably happen, then the creation of a supranational State and power will be very likely, and "European programming," already being actively prepared, will have a good chance of becoming reality.

An important part of the "democratic left" and certain Chris-

[5] Notably if protest against the EEC takes place as a coordinated, organized action by the labor movements (unions and parties) of several neighboring nations (within the EEC or not), with the aim of creating a community of socialist states which would evidently not be limited to the European continent. But this eventuality is something quite different from the "national withdrawal" which is favored by a part of the working class movement, especially in France. It presupposes an alternative policy of European integration, and not the pure and simple rejection of integration altogether.

tian labor leaders call on the working class to support this solution, confronting it with the following dilemma: either the labor movement allies itself with European technocracy in order to impose "planning" on big business and on the German liberals, or else there will be no planning at all and we will foot the bill.

Put in these terms, the alternatives are unacceptable. One cannot expect from "European planning" as it is now envisaged any modification of the purposes and the orientations of the capitalist economy. On the contrary, as the present proponents of this idea understand it, its purpose is to achieve on the supranational level that "integration of the labor movement" into capitalist institutions which is being tried without much success on the domestic level by the partisans of economic consensus. Within the framework of present social and economic structures they want to bring workers' and employers' organizations together to work out jointly a "plan" having quasi-legal status, it being understood that this plan will neither overthrow existing structures nor in any way encroach on the power of the employers and capitalists with whom the workers are "in consensus." The labor movement's "participation" in this plan, in a subordinate position, tends to "countervail" the employer's demands, agreed; but it also tends to reinforce the capitalist State's position as mediator and arbitrator, and above all to trap the labor movement into accepting solutions which conform to capitalist logic, which have been worked out "together," and which cannot therefore be questioned later on.

If it accepted such a formula, the labor movement would obviously make a fool's bargain. "Cooperative planning" on the international level would be even more unfavorable than it is on the domestic level. In the latter instance, at least, the labor movement still can *at the moment* influence the course of negotiations by mass actions to which the State and the employers are immediately sensitive. If, on the other hand, these negotiations take place in Brussels or in Luxembourg, the balance of power swings in favor of the employers: in effect, they have the power of immediate decision, they dispose of a stable chain of command, and the requirements and the inertia of permanent structures (fixed capital and money) work in their favor, while the power of the workers' representatives is effective only to the degree that the workers are mobilized and militant at a given moment. Cut off from the working masses, having to make decisions whose terms or meanings are often objectionable or unknown to the masses, the workers' representatives are under strong pressure to become technocrats among other technocrats, working out summit compromises which win a great deal less than mass action could have. European planning as presently conceived is a new attempt to deprive the labor movement on the international level of the weapons which it still wields on the national level, and to enmesh it in capitalist logic.

It is therefore absurd to want to have the working class follow the lead of European technocracy on the pretext that capitalist planning is better than no planning at all. Planning is not an end in itself, nor is the strengthening of governmental powers, be they national or supranational. These measures interest the working class only to the degree that they expose and sharpen the contradiction between the social character of production and the private ownership of its means, between economic desirability and capitalist profitability, between social needs and financial interests. They are interesting only to the degree that they permit a change in the balance of power and a step forward in the struggle of the masses toward objectives which undermine capitalist power and ever more concretely foreshadow the nature and the necessity of socialist solutions.

Can European integration provide the working class with fruitful opportunities for attack? Can these attacks be carried out if need be when supranational "planning" goes into effect? Can and should the working class movement seize the initiative by beginning here and now to fight for European economic planning not dominated by the power of capital? Should it instead fight against the establishment of supranational regulation, considering such measures as weapons aimed at the working class? Or should it stand back and wait to see which turn events will take?

Before attempting to outline an answer to these questions, I shall examine the principal problems and contradictions which the pursuit of European integration will create.

3. *Regional Crises*

The merger of economies so uncomplementary and so deeply engaged in competition as those of Western Europe could have no chance of success except on the condition that "conditions of competition" in all the countries of the EEC be more or less equalized with every step toward integration. That means that the various elements of production costs should not be affected by governmental intervention, e.g., public subsidies to manufacturing and service industries, including transportation, which would be contrary to the rules of free competition and the laws of the market. It also means that the costs added to the price of a product by the social, economic, and fiscal policy of the different governments (social security, taxation, credit policy) should be the same everywhere.

A "harmonization" of fiscal, social, and monetary policies, as well as of energy and transport policies, is therefore a necessary precondition of this plan. Publicly owned industries must operate according to the rules of capitalist enterprise, and governmental subsidies must as much as possible disappear. Where suppression of subsidies is altogether impossible (principally in agriculture), common policies must be worked out.

These guiding principles were obviously conceived within the classic liberal perspective. To postulate that private enterprises should be placed in identical positions by the respective governments insofar as their production costs depend on governmental policy is to neglect at the outset the diversity of social problems which capitalist initiative and expansion have created in countries with very different populations, structures, and levels of development.

It was therefore predictable that the "harmonization" of the different governments' policies and the abandonment of state intervention would tend to aggravate social and regional disparities, that the withdrawal of protection from certain essentially regional industries (coal mining in the North of France or Belgium, shipyards, metal industries of outlying regions) would end by ruining them, and the economic decline of these regions could not be counteracted by private industrial development or reconversion efforts because, in a liberal economy, private industry could not become competitive in declining regions. Nor could public initiative help to bring these regions out of their age-long impoverishment and underdevelopment, because the cost of large public development efforts would necessarily increase the fiscal burden carried by private enterprise and, therefore, the latter's production costs.

At the same time, the decline of certain regions (especially Wallonia and the Mezzogiorno) risked provoking repercussions on the economies of the nations concerned, as well as tensions and centrifugal tendencies which might endanger the cohesion of the EEC. Thus European technocrats cite the regional imbalances provoked by monopolist expansion, even more than over-investment and distortion, as a compelling argument in favor of "European planning."

According to figures published by the Executive of the EEC, "industrial Lotharingia," plus the Rhône and Po valleys, represents 60 per cent of the EEC's industrial production, but only 45 per cent of its population and 35 per cent of its territory. At a conference on the subject of "planning" in the Common Market, held in Rome in September 1962, the Socialist deputy Giolitti[6] emphasized that the Common Market had established a "superstructure" while at the same time creating structural problems which the individual governments are less and less equipped to solve. Because of its liberal principles, the Treaty of Rome, while it hopes for "balanced development," in effect abandons the responsibility of creating equilibrium to the laws of the market, that is to say the laws of capitalist profit. It hopes that the pursuit of maximum returns from invested capital will by itself create the most rational division of labor between nations, regions, and private groups. It extends only temporary approval to the timid interventions carried out by the French government which, through special depreciation allowances, tax exemptions, partial wage subsidies, and finan-

[6] The Italian Socialist Party (PSI—*Partito Socialista Italiano*). [Publisher's note.]

cial support to the railroads, tries to attract private industry into depressed regions and thereby to create artificial and temporary conditions for profitable investment.

The ineffectiveness of this type of public incentive has already been largely demonstrated. While direct or indirect government subsidies may guarantee normal or above normal profits for a few years to the companies in the declining regions who benefit from these measures, such inducements are not enough to attract serious entrepreneurs and to keep them there. These inducements will end one day, but the disadvantages or handicaps inherent in the situation will remain. When public inducements do seem to have some success (tire industry in the North, Remington at Caluire, etc.), the reason is most often that the depressed region offered geographic or logistic advantages for industry quite apart from government inducements. It is one thing to establish an industry in the North, in Alsace or in the Rhône valley; but it is quite another thing to establish one in Corrèze, in the Vendée, or in Lucanie. There are as yet no examples of important industrial investments in these latter regions. The only effort of some importance to industrialize a declining region has taken place in the Mezzogiorno, according to the strategy of development "poles," to which we shall return. But the few results that have been obtained there were always due to the collectivity, either because the IRI (*Istituto per la Ricostruzione Industriale*, a State-owned holding company) created industries with very long-term public financing, or because the Italian government paid a substantial part (about half, for example, in the case of the Montecatini plant at Brindisi) of the private firm's construction and installation costs, and also financed through non-refundable loans the necessary infrastructure (railroad or harbor connections, local improvements, landscaping, housing, public transportation).

The closer one looks the more one sees that the rules of free competition and the free play of prices within the laws of the market are violated everywhere. Whether one deals with underdeveloped regions or with growing, highly industrialized zones, it is always the collectivity which guarantees the profitability of invested capital by assuming the social costs of "free enterprise."

These social costs of monopoly expansion and of private enterprise include training of manpower, developmental planning (road building and urbanization), public transportation (city and suburban), the general expenses of urbanization: supply of energy and water, anti-pollution measures, hygiene and public health, social welfare) as well as the economic cost of emigration from declining regions ("desertification," fiscal deficit in public and administrative services, social relief, devaluation of property).

We shall again have occasion to speak of the fact that when one considers the social cost of the geographic concentration of industrial activity and the abandonment of outlying, resource-poor regions, then this kind of concentration does not have that economic rationality which bourgeois economists often attribute to it. What we wish to emphasize at the moment is that everywhere and under all conditions the degree to which private investment yields a profit depends either directly or indirectly on government intervention, on the manner in which the State pays for the social cost, and general expense of private initiative. Once that is understood it becomes clear that the laissez-faire and free market competitive practices imposed as a superstructure by the Common Market require the harmonization of precisely the same measures of government intervention, including fiscal, monetary, and financial policies, which at the same time are supposed to be subordinated to the market economy.

The contradictions and conflicts which these efforts at harmonization must create become immediately evident. Since social as well as private production costs are linked to fiscal pressure among other things, a harmonization of fiscal policies is necessarily on the agenda. For instance, the public resources required by the different governments to carry out their economic interventions differ from one country to another. For example, the requirements of the Italian government, which has to deal with the problems of the Mezzogiorno, South-North migrations, social backwardness, demographic pressures, etc., are *a priori* proportionately higher than those of Belgium, where a relative demographic and industrial stagnation prevails, or of West Germany. At the same time the desire to attract foreign investment and to further self-financing of domestic companies leads the Italian government—despite its great need for revenue—to reduce its fiscal pressure on capitalist groups to a minimum. What is more, the poorest communities of the Mezzogiorno, those which therefore have the greatest need for public resources in order to develop socially and economically, grant the most favorable conditions in order to attract industrial firms (and the trusts, by the way, organize competitive bidding among the most impoverished communities). This process has two consequences:

1. In the interest of not discriminating fiscally against the capitalist groups of a relatively less developed country in favor of their foreign competitors, and in the interest of attracting investments into underdeveloped regions by means of para-fiscal inducements, the State loses the means necessary to stimulate the development of these regions. Essentially, it abandons this task to capitalist initiative, with the consequences which we shall discuss below. In Italy as in France, the disparities between North and South or (in France) East and West, are growing continually despite a few spectacular successes in the Mezzogiorno.

2. Even if all of its profits are reinvested productively, capitalist accumulation diverts resources which might have furthered social development or covered priority needs, and it diverts them toward short-term profitable activities. The result, in underdeveloped regions which experience a relative upswing, is the same phenomenon of "slummification" as in colonies or semi-colonies: misery with television sets, illiteracy with transistor radios, slums with private cars.

Indeed any economic policy (necessarily a planned policy which attempts to diminish or wipe out regional disparities) collides and will long continue to collide with the laws of monopoly competition. For if the degree of monopoly enjoyed by each industrial corporation has declined relative to the Common Market as a whole, its economic and political power has nevertheless increased within each individual nation. When the State wants industries to be transferred to or established in underdeveloped regions, the monopolies can answer that competition compels them to pursue the maximum return from their investment, and if they choose to locate their investments according to any other criteria they risk losing (and making their country lose) their position in international competition. The example of Remington's abandonment of its factory in Caluire, which had been constructed with government subsidies, and its transfer to more favorable locations (the Netherlands and Italy) illustrates the ineffectiveness of these public inducements. The example of Neyrpic in Grenoble shows that even a domestic firm can go against the wishes of the planners by preparing the transfer of its factories to another location (Belfort) where they would be more profitable, thus dealing a fatal blow to the long-term development plan of the region (Rhône-Alpes).

Only public enterprises could resist the tendency toward geographic concentration, inasmuch as public capital is available to them on better terms than on the financial market, and only public enterprises could enjoy autonomous initiative in coordination with autonomous regional bodies. It is evident that the volume of capital necessary to counteract the "spontaneous" line of monopoly development will become available only if the accumulation of capital is regulated in the public interest, which presupposes both an effective nationalization of credit and a different economic orientation than that imposed by monopoly capital. The European Development Bank, whose activity remains purely symbolic, cannot possibly be effective in this sense. First of all, its endowment is much too small. Second, it is by definition free from democratic, regional, and local control, and its activity—even if it had more funds—would necessarily be guided by technocratic and financial criteria, which tend to follow a neo-colonialist model of development instead of revitalizing declining regions by means of balanced development. And incidentally, the different national technocracies, as well as European technocracy in general, are, despite certain reservations about the "gadget civilization," partisans of the American model of development, with its "megalopolis" and its deserts, and its satisfaction of "conditioned" private needs to the detriment not only of "pockets of misery" but also of elementary, social needs.

While the aggravation of regional disparities and imbalances confronts the member states of the EEC with growing problems, the intra-community monopoly competition at the same time hinders the different national planning organs from finding or applying progressive solutions. In theory, of course, supranational planning and a European budget would make it possible to fight against increasing disparities and to counteract and reduce the effects of monopolist expansion. But in practice it is difficult to imagine a European technocracy with enough freedom of action vis-à-vis the national governments from which it derives to be perceptibly more independent and progressive than they. Thus at the same time that the Common Market creates the necessity for more effective regional planning, it hinders this planning, at least in its present phase; and it resists decentralization and regional autonomy, which are the essential preconditions of harmonious development.

4. *The Agricultural Crisis*

The extension of the Common Market to the agricultural sector has raised the hope (so far unfulfilled) of an international division of labor favoring the regions with well established agriculture to the detriment of those which because of natural or *social* conditions (one must insist on the latter) cannot hope to have competitive production costs.

The prospect of a division of agricultural production and markets has accelerated a two-fold process which had begun even before 1957:

—Mechanization and rationalization of methods;

—Capitalist concentration and vertical integration of agriculture by trusts located both on the production side (processed foods, and industrial products necessary for agriculture) and on the distribution side (canning, capitalist commerce) of agriculture.

Especially in Italy and France this double process has created a considerable acceleration of the rural exodus. In eight years France has "lost" one fourth of its agricultural population, and Italy nearly one third in ten years.

A rural exodus of such proportions cannot by itself and in general be considered as economically rational and socially beneficial. I do not deny that ten years ago the agricultural structure of most French and Italian regions was archaic, nor that before the massive exodus the rural areas were overpopulated. Nor do I deny the fact that modern production techniques can be useful only over areas which are usually far larger than the family farm, especially the small plots which were the rule under the archaic system of land tenure. It is also clear that agricultural concentration and a fairly large rural exodus were necessary. These developments freed a large number of peasants from a job which was all the more difficult and unrewarding because it had to be done by hand (the plots being too small for mechanization), and allowed those who remained on the land to work larger areas with more modern methods, realizing greater yields.

But what I do question is the rationality, both economic and human, of the manner in which these governments with their moderate liberalism are going about the task not of *solving* the agricultural problem but of *eliminating* it. Even at first sight it would seem that the rationalization of agriculture requires particularly strict planning, including especially:

—A quantitative and qualitative study of markets;

—The organization of production and of markets (especially for perishables) on the national as well as regional and local levels in such a way as to obtain the optimum adjustment of supply and demand;

—A large amount of funds for the purpose of financing reorganization, conversion, modernization, and mechanization;

—A program of education and job training for the young people and *the adults* who are leaving the land;

—A system of agricultural retirement pensions in order to guarantee that the exodus does not consist primarily of young people, leaving the remaining land in the hands of people who are prevented by their old age from keeping it going;

—A reform of the land tenure system for the purpose of facilitating reorganization, and cooperative methods;

—Local and regional industrialization programs, beginning with the agricultural, food, and related industries, in order to employ the surplus agricultural labor force as much as possible in its home region, and also for the purpose of furthering control by the producers over the various industrial processing steps of their products, as well as over the development of their region and community.

Not one of these conditions has been completely or, often, even partially fulfilled. The profound transformations necessary in agriculture have essentially been abandoned to the care of private initiative, with the following consequences:

—Anarchy of production and markets, even in non-perishables, with a series of scarcities and surpluses which facilitate speculative maneuvers by intermediaries;

—Capitalist concentration, the creation of a profitable agricultural big business; domination of agricultural production, considered simply as a source of raw materials to be transformed and sold at a profit, by the industrial and commercial trusts;

—The rush of the rural masses, most of them young and unskilled, toward the traditional industrial centers, with the resulting depopulation of entire regions *below the threshold of economic viability*.

Incapable of solving the problem of backward rural regions, capitalism is in the process of eliminating it by condemning these regions to death. Most of them, Apulia and Sicily for example, but also South Central France, are not lacking in natural wealth, actual or potential; their decline is due above all to centuries of under-investment or of capital export, and (as far as the regions of the Mezzogiorno are concerned) to centuries of feudal parasitism. The elimination of these regions is not an economic necessity; it arises from the fact that *under present conditions* the return from agricultural investment in these regions is lower than what can be obtained in other regions and in other sectors. But the differences in return are short term financial ones, in the narrowest sense: indeed, the conditions of profitability, while they are not already present in these regions, can be created by long-term investments, whose economic value (and financial unprofitability) is analogous to that of investments in research, education, or the nuclear industry.

The economic value of these investments, which must of

necessity be public, is a subject of old controversies. Those who favor the "megalopolis" and the elimination of underdeveloped regions emphasize that the greater profitability of investments outside these regions is an *economic* argument; their adversaries, among whom I count myself, contend the contrary. It is a demonstrable fact that the greater profitability of investments in developed regions can be maintained only by massive public investments to create an urban infrastructure, and, if one takes into account the cost of this infrastructure and the quantity of public and private services which it makes necessary, then an unskilled worker who emigrates from Bretagne to Paris or from Apulia to Milan is relatively less productive in the big city. And finally it can be demonstrated that the complete depopulation of rural regions creates in time a series of evils (such as soil erosion and "desertification," which generate climatic and hydrological changes) whose tragic effects will spread to neighboring regions if the costly task of preventing them is not undertaken.

In truth, to decide in favor of the "megalopolis" is at bottom to make a political decision in favor of "free enterprise" and against any public and planned redistribution of resources and investment, a redistribution which would tend to give preponderance to the public sector, to make investment a public function and responsibility, a responsibility guided by long-term economic and human criteria—criteria which are, as we have seen, incompatible with the profit economy.

The limits which the ideology of the Common Market imposes on governmental action are particularly conspicuous in this domain. Regional planning in the EEC is handled by a commission with anemic resources. The members of this commission cannot go very far beyond the projects of the national governments; their task, in any case, cannot be to look first for the optimum economic solution to regional problems and then to adjust and correct these solutions in the light of coherent supranational optimum criteria. Their task is limited to ensuring the coherence of the different national projects, and they have little or no possibility of influencing the qualitative and political orientation of the latter. Where regional problems are concerned, therefore, one cannot expect better solutions from supranational "planning" than from the already very insufficient national "planning."

It is true, on the other hand, that the Common Market has increased the necessity for public regulation of the volume of agricultural production. The supply-demand equilibrium is not left in the hands of the "regulating mechanisms" of the market in the EEC any more than it is in the United States. Price supports, government purchase and storage of surpluses, and collective financing of agricultural exports to countries outside the EEC are included among the principles of the EEC's agricultural policy. The creation of a common agricultural market with an international division of labor and equalization of price guarantees are measures which precisely conflict with the governmental regulations now in force and with the contradictory interests of the member states. The common agricultural market requires on the one hand that the EEC be nearly autonomous agriculturally, that is to say, that the overall volume of production in the EEC be adjusted to the overall volume of demand; but, on the other hand, the EEC's free exchange and free competition principles results in the projection of geographical specialization, which would further accelerate the rural exodus from the less favored regions. Because these regions are much more numerous and more densely populated in West Germany and in Italy than in France and the Netherlands, the EEC-wide desire to maintain a large middle peasantry for purposes of social and political "stabilization" is in contradiction with this same desire on the part of the governments.

Furthermore, West Germany, which transacts only 40 per cent of its trade with the other countries of the EEC, intends to defend its farmers by guaranteeing high prices, to protect its industrial outlets outside of the EEC by continuing to buy agricultural products in third countries, and to keep its industrial production costs down by importing low priced agricultural products, all at the same time. (The American prices, with or without dumping, are lower than the EEC price could be, even if the latter were based on the French prices, which is incidentally out of the questin.) The result is that West Germany—and Italy and the Netherlands to a lesser degree—offers apparently contradictory arguments (the necessity for high prices to defend its peasantry, the necessity to import cheaply from outside the EEC to defend its balance of payments and its internal prices) against the agricultural Common Market, which, unlike the industrial Common Market, would require a relatively rigorous quantitative and qualitative national and supranational plan.

At the moment it seems that the EEC is moving toward a hybrid compromise including everything for everybody: guaranteed high prices for the farmers within the EEC, continued imports from the United States, and collective financing of the agricultural surpluses (mostly from France) which the two previous circumstances will certainly increase. This incoherent compromise would multiply the disadvantages. On the one hand it would perpetuate agricultural surpluses on two highly industrialized continents (North America and Western Europe, and perhaps later on Australia also), which is not only an economic absurdity but also facilitates the now classic utilization of these surpluses for neo-colonialist foreign policy purposes.[7] On the other hand, and

[7] In nearly all of the underdeveloped countries, food deficits and endemic hunger *are not due to natural causes but to social and political causes:* barter exchanges of low-priced agricultural products for high-priced industrial products, monoculture, feudalism, usury. Land reform implying social revolution would make a solution to the food problem possible everywhere.

If the developed capitalist countries envisage covering the agricultural deficits of the "Third World" by food grants indefinitely, their purpose is to prevent peasant revolutions (or any revolutions at all) according to the Chinese model. As far as the working class movement is concerned, the supplying of agricultural products to the "Third World" should therefore only be a transitory form of assistance to help the underdeveloped countries *get started*. This aid should not continually increase; it should diminish, to be replaced by industrial and technical aid consisting principally of producer goods (and especially of goods which permit the production of producer goods).

However, a non-colonialist aid policy must under no circumstances consist of giving to underdeveloped countries at first the most technically advanced industrial apparatus. The arbitrary infusion of this kind of industry into societies prostrated by unemployment, underemployment, and malnutrition is, on the contrary, neo-colonialist. This kind of injection destroys the civilization and the autonomy of the "receiving" country; it leads to the birth of a technical and labor aristocracy which is cut off from the masses,

despite the preceding, it would permit the continued economic and social decay of declining regions, and the intensification of regional disparities.

From the preceding exposition one can see fairly clearly how strong the contradictions between different national interests are in the agricultural sector, and how numerous are the traps which await the peasant movement, even a movement inspired by socialism. Thus, a "community-wide" agricultural plan, certain premises of which were contained in the partial agreements of January 1962 (without, however, having really been applied up to now), tends to be favored by the French peasantry, the most "European" of them all, because it believes that through the Common Market it can enlarge its markets and get higher prices, to the detriment of the agricultural producers of other countries. Inversely, the steadfast defense of West German and Italian agriculture, especially the grain farmers, could succeed only on two conditions:

1. If it kept the agricultural Common Market from becoming a reality, which would have the result of continuing and even increasing the purchases of American grain;

---

and to the intensification of social disparities, the continuation of unemployment, and sub-proletarization (or "slummification").

The great lesson of the Chinese revolution (see especially the writings of René Dumont, Frantz Fanon, and Enrica Collotti-Pischel) is that economic and social development must be carried out by the masses themselves. It must be carried out by the *progressive* achievement and elevation of the technological level, by the construction of an individualized and original culture, which begins by utilizing already existing human and natural resources. Economic aid from industrially advanced countries, as important as it is (especially in the construction of primary industries: mining, energy, fertilizer, steel), must necessarily play a marginal role.

The desire to deny inequalities in development or to call for their elimination arises from an idealist and voluntarist interpretation of proletarian internationalism.

The contradiction between the developed world and the underdeveloped world is a reality which inevitably expresses itself on the ideological level (as the Sino-Soviet conflict shows); neither ideology nor sentiment can overcome it. Proletarian internationalism does not consist of denying the existence of this contradiction; it does consist of preventing this contradiction from becoming opposition. (See my introduction to the special issue of *Les Temps Modernes* on the Sino-Soviet dispute, May 1963.)

2. If a "community-wide" price were established close to the Italian or German price.

Now in the first case, the small and medium French producers would suffer because they would be smothered by the surplus; in the second case, the "community's" surpluses would reach a crushing volume, which would have to be shipped out to the detriment of the countries of the Third World, and which would create in France a situation analogous to that of American agriculture.

The socialist answer to this set of problems cannot be to defend all small and medium farms everywhere and at all costs, nor even to defend the present overall level of the agricultural population. Instead of waging a defensive battle to keep the poor farmers on their land, it would be better to wage an offensive struggle for the industrial and cultural reorganization and development of depressed agricultural regions, a development which will open up new productive possibilities (dairy products, vegetables, fruits, and forests) which at present are lacking in these regions themselves.

CHAPTER TWO

Europe for the Workers

We asked ourselves at the beginning of this investigation if there were complementarity or contradiction between the processes begun or accelerated by the Common Market on the one hand and the necessity for planning which arises out of these processes on the other hand. We might have said *a priori* that this contradiction does not exist. Capitalist planning exists for the express purpose of maintaining the existing social relationships and orientations, of consolidating capitalism by rationalizing it, and, by coordinating private and public decisions, of reducing the inherent risks of private initiative.

Although that is indeed the purpose of the projected plans on the national and supra-national levels, it is impossible to assert *a priori* that this goal can be achieved—that in other words European capitalism can solve the problems created by economic integration and reinforce and consolidate itself at the same time. We believe that either one or the other will happen: either it will try to eliminate and to elude these problems by returning, in the spirit of the Treaty of Rome, to the classic forms of free exchange and private initiative, and will therefore expose itself to the dangers of cyclical fluctuation and to social tensions which will prevent it from continuing on that road; or it will try to correct its most serious cyclical fluctuations and distortions by means of reformist planning and thus to make monopolist expansion socially tolerable—in which case it will be led to call for public intervention which although endeavoring to maintain the system, nevertheless will open breaches therein into which a strong and conscious labor movement may throw itself to challenge the entire system. (In practice, the alternatives are not so clear cut: laissez-faire, which generates social tensions, and reformist planning, which offers the Left opportunities to attack, coexist in variable proportions.)

In any case, during the coming decade the European class struggle will be shaped by European economic integration in whatever form it takes, and by the upheavals which will accompany the process of the internationalization of production on all levels. We should therefore examine what possibilities for action offer themselves to the working class, and we should begin by eliminating those developments which at present seem out of the question. The following developments seem to us to fall into that category:

1. *The return to national protectionism*—Certain working class organizations (the PCF and the CGT especially) were still quite recently reluctant to raise the question of a supranational struggle against the Common Market, the question of an alternative to capitalist integration, or of what one may call "antagonistic participation" in the supranational institutions. This reluctance seems to be motivated by the desire not to recognize European integration (in the sense of "recognizing" a government) by working out a strategy which tries to benefit from this integration, which attempts to intervene in its processes to change their orientation and their nature. Such a strategy would imply in effect *accepting* European integration as an accomplished, irreversible fact. Inversely, to refuse to consider such a strategy implies that one continues to count on a sudden, premature end of the experiment.

We have already said that in the intermediate range the failure of European integration was not to be excluded, and that this eventuality would present the working class movement with real possibilities of intervention, although under unenviable conditions and with unattractive long-term prospects.

On the other hand, no matter how the EEC overcomes (or is destroyed by) its next crisis, the tendency toward the internationalization of production is an objective process linked to the dimensions, the degree of specialization, and the cost of a productive apparatus (regardless of whether it is capitalist or socialist) which incorporates modern technology.

In the long run a return to national protectionism and to economic nationalism is therefore to be excluded as a possibility. It can be considered as a socialist goal or a socialist solution neither economically nor politically. Without thereby accepting the framework, the limits, and the nature of the "Europe" which is now under construction, a more fruitful strategy would be to investigate by what means the working class, by intervening antagonistically in this construction, can take over the process of internationalization and guide it according to its wishes, both by fighting on the all-European level for an anti-monopolistic integration process and by organizing international counter-powers outside of existing institutions.

2. *A catastrophic crisis in part or all of the EEC or capitalist world*—To the degree that each capitalist economy (inside as well as outside the EEC) depends on its foreign markets, it is sensitive to the economic fluctuation of its customer-states. This mutual dependence will increase with the development of intercapitalist exchange and with the withdrawal of protective tariffs from the individual national economies. The stabilizing measures of the different states will lose their effectiveness and the liberal spirit of the Treaty of Rome will blunt their instruments. A supranational policy is being worked out now precisely for that reason. The effectiveness of this policy will be limited, but it will be sufficient to avoid deeper depressions than those which the United States—which is much less well equipped in this regard than the countries of the EEC—has experienced beginning in 1958.

3. *The preservation or the reestablishment of the free play of competition and of a competitive market*—This goal, which is part of the program of the German Social Democrats among others, is already outmoded and therefore illusory. It cannot be considered as an answer (or as an answer from the Left) to monopoly capitalism. Perfect competition is dead, if it ever existed. Monopolist and oligopolist competition is the prevailing reality. This competition does not revolve around the satisfaction of needs (of course, needs which cannot be translated into *individual* market demand, are eliminated from the outset); it deals instead with the marginal differences between mass produced goods which industry offers to the consumers' desires. No arsenal of antitrust laws can put an end to the subordination of consumption to production, the domination of the economy by the pursuit of profit, and the resulting

inversion of real priorities. The concentration of economic power in a limited number of centers of decision making is an irreversible tendency of modern capitalism.

Even if the EEC were to dilute itself into an "Atlantic" free exchange zone it would be rapidly dominated by the monopolies and the cartels, while private and public regulation would tend to make monopoly competition socially tolerable and to guarantee sufficient profits for the monopolies to pursue their expansion.

All this does not mean, evidently, that the concentration and internationalization of production and economic power should be passively accepted. It means only that instead of denouncing abstractly the processes and changes which are under way and hoping thus to bring them to a halt, the workers' struggle will be more effective if it succeeds in demonstrating on the various levels of economic and social changes the necessity and the possibility of anti-monopolist solutions which move in a socialist direction. Rather than waging an impossible frontal assault against the existence of the Common Market and of economic integration, there should be worked out, in my opinion, a strategy of partial and coordinated struggles whose objective is to present a democratic alternative to the Europe of the cartels and the trusts.

1. *The Levels of the Struggle*

The principal levels on which the working classes can, in my opinion, intervene in the ongoing changes in order to modify the general orientation of capitalist society by changing the partial and local structures and power relationships include:

A) *The Company, the Occupation, the Job*

Monopolist concentration and competition, *but also the development of technology*, create reconversion, readjustment, and employment problems in most sectors; problems which capitalism tends to solve in its own way, that is to say by ignoring the needs of the workers and of the population in the sectors or regions which are being reorganized. The answer given by the working class or by the peasantry cannot be identical where a structural crisis common to all industrial societies is concerned (the coal crisis, the shipbuilding or wheat growing crisis) and where the crisis is due to the financial strategies of the monopolies. We shall therefore examine these two types of crises separately.

"The organization of industry," Pierre Belleville writes, "takes place these days according to the rules of capitalist concentration. When a trust takes over control of an important but hitherto relatively independent company, its purpose is not necessarily to take over its profits. Its purpose can also be to 'clean up' the production sector which it dominates by neutralizing the industrial potential represented by this company." [1] The crises experienced by Neyrpic, Remington, and General Motors at Gennevilliers, for example, fall into this category. So does the emasculation experienced by numerous companies in mechanical construction, pharmaceutical products, electronics, and aviation, who in falling under the control of (usually foreign) trusts become servile copiers of the patents and designs of the larger company, and abandoning all research activity, undertake personnel layoffs beginning with their most highly skilled workers. A kind of scientific neo-colonialism preserves for the larger company (American, Dutch, British) the tasks of invention and directing production, while the subsidiary is assigned the task of execution. Deprived of all autonomy, either scientific or economic, these subsidiaries are used to absorb the shocks of cyclical business fluctuations, and their employees will be among the first to feel them.

Researchers, technicians, skilled workers, and students are the first to suffer from this relationship of subordination and dependence which disqualifies them professionally, destroys the intellectual and cultural autonomy toward which they legitimately aspire, and deprives them of the full development of their abilities. Concretely or potentially, their interest is the same as that of all the other workers who have received from the trust, especially in its most recent plants, no more that a "house qualification," which keeps them tied forever to "their" company because their skills are worthless elsewhere. The defense of their jobs and their professional autonomy in these cases necessitates the defense of the

[1] *Une Nouvelle Classe Ouvrière*, Chapter 5.

autonomy of their company, or when the latter is part of a really overcrowded sector (the case of General Motors in Gennevilliers) it requires a fight for the socialization of the investment function and the reorientation of investment and production according to real needs. For example, in the case of the pharmaceutical industry, which is particularly threatened because of its dispersion, the socialization of the entire industry is necessary together with the transfer into public research centers of the numerous scientists and researchers who perform routine maintenance tasks in this industry. This is necessary both to reanimate a publicly essential industry and to put an end to the exploitation of the Social Security program by the trusts, most of them foreign. Likewise, in the scientific industries (Neyrpic, for example), only a nationalization which respects the autonomy of the individual companies can prevent the destruction of their research potential, which according to short-term financial criteria does not pay.

In industries which are undergoing a structural crisis, on the other hand, the defense of jobs and occupation can hardly take the form of the defense of companies destined to be shut down or reconverted. Already in dealing with agriculture we have seen that the defense of the Italian and German grain growers would amount to an attack against their counterparts in France and in other countries. In the same way the defense of the coal mining areas of South Central France or of the Borinage region would—in the absence of a policy radically different from that of the CECA[2]—throw the weight of the coal crisis onto the German and Dutch miners (and the British, Polish, and American). To the degree that the coal crisis, like the shipbuilding and textile crises, is a world-wide phenomenon, the working class is beaten from the outset if it restricts itself to defensive battles. The struggle for jobs and for the utilization of human and natural resources must necessarily be offensive: the working class must oppose its own reconversion and reorganization plan to that of the technocrats; it must demand the power of control over these questions; it must

[2] The European Coal and Steel Community (CECA—*Communauté Européenne du Charbon et de l'Acier*), created in 1957. [Publisher's note.]

fight on that basis. It must be able to show concretely that the reconversion problem can be solved. The solution cannot be found by keeping decrepit mines and shipyards in operation by rear guard battles. But it can be found, for example, by the extension and development toward organic chemistry and the pharmaceutical industry of a nationalized coal industry, and by the transformation of the shipyards into public mechanical construction enterprises. And it must be able to show that the only obstacle to this kind of solution, a solution which corresponds to the resources of the respective regions, is the present desire of the capitalist State to restrict its activities to deficit producing sectors, and to reserve profitable and expanding sectors for private enterprise, whose profits normally ought to cover the cost of reconversion and of social development.

On the basis of a concrete reconversion and development plan which challenges the State's economic policy and the monopolies' centralizing strategy, the working class will be able to attract and mobilize other strata of the population who are equally interested in having the declining industries—which almost always have a regional character—replaced by other industries with good futures, and in preventing a general decline in the region. The necessity for reconversions thus offers the working class the opportunity to intervene actively in the process of transformation. The elaboration of regional and sectoral objectives which confront and oppose the strategy of the monopolies and the technocracies is the starting point for an "alternative" policy and of democratic planning moving toward socialism.

B) *The Region*

We have already indicated the ineffectiveness, in part intentional, of the regional policy of State capitalism and we have traced the outlines of a regional model of development which should be opposed to the policy of "development poles" and of the employment monopoly which the latter most often confers on newly established trusts.

The battle for the balanced development of "eccentric" regions can be fought around a certain number of mobilizing themes:

1. The battle for schools and for the independence of the schools from big business, which tends to annex them on the pretext of providing job training;

2. The battle for the creation of public industrial enterprises according to a regional development program worked out by democratically elected regional assemblies under regional control;

3. Battles against the exploitation of peasants by intermediaries and by the trusts who sell to them at retail prices and buy from them at gross prices, and in favor of the development of cooperative production, mechanization, industrial processing, and distribution of agricultural products;

4. The struggle for low interest loans for machinery, for reconversion, for the creation of cooperatives.

c) *The Alternative*

The workers' partial struggles for jobs and wages, for the proper valuing of human and natural resources, for control over working conditions, and for the social satisfaction of the social needs created by industrial civilization, cannot succeed unless they are guided by an alternative social model on the political level, a model which gives these partial battles a comprehensive perspective. This alternative model, whose implementation presupposes the political hegemony of the working class, serves as reference, as framework, and as unifying mediation for the various partial demands which, without such a model, cannot go beyond the reformist ideology nor escape absorption into the system. This model, or "democratic alternative" to monopoly planning, must not be conceived out of a love for opposition at any price, as a list of demands to be presented "because" capitalism is unable to satisfy them. Quite the contrary, it must be presented as the *meaning* of the struggles which are already under way, as the positive image of an autonomy which the working class asserts for the moment in a negative and partial manner (as a challenge).

In short, we must oppose capitalist planning, which is essentially quantitative, and which conceives production as an end in itself and society as a means, with a qualitative plan which conceives production as a means to satisfy real, autonomous needs.

These needs, contrary to the assertions of capitalist planning, cannot appear on the market, either because those to whose needs these demands correspond are not solvent, or, even if they were solvent, because the conditions for the satisfaction of these demands are not present, because to create these conditions is not profitable from the capitalist viewpoint.

Among the most important of these needs are the needs for public services and facilities, made necessary by the development of the productive forces—for example: education, health, hygiene, city planning, housing, public transportation, cultural and athletic facilities, research, and information. In an advanced society, in which the mode and the process of production require the maintenance of at least the appearance of democratic liberties, the satisfaction of these needs can hardly be left in the hands of free enterprise, that is to say the individual profitable sale of the necessary services. These needs are essentially *social:* they are not generally translatable into individual demand and cannot be satisfied by commercial services based on the "liberty" of selling to the highest bidder and the "liberty" of not buying at that price.

The satisfaction of these needs is imperative and should be given priority because upon it depends both the human tolerability of the society and the reproduction of labor power—the simple reproduction: health, hygiene, city planning, and housing; and the wider reproduction: education, research, information, and cultural facilities. Satisfying these needs represents what one may call the "general social costs" of private initiative. These needs, indeed, are at least potentially creative and cultural. The degree and manner in which they are satisfied depends upon the degree to which human abilities are allowed to develop and the degree to which life and social relationships are "humanized."

Because the satisfaction of these needs does not further capitalist accumulation and is unprofitable, it is left in the hands of the State and is entered on the debit side of the national budget: that is to say, in the category of unproductive expenditures. Capitalism has no spontaneous interest whatsoever in satisfying these needs[3] because their necessarily social satisfaction (by means of public services) (a) diverts toward the social sector, through taxation and fiscal pressure, a portion of surplus values which otherwise could have been consumed or reinvested at a profit; and (b) diverts toward social consumption a portion of individual buying power which otherwise would have flowed into the cash registers of private companies.

It is therefore in the interests of the latter to limit social consumption as far as possible and to subordinate it quantitatively and qualitatively to the criteria of private accumulation. Furthermore, because the centers of capital accumulation and the utilization of the surplus are controlled by private capitalists,[4] because the cost of a gigantic apparatus of commercial propaganda is considered as a deductible expenditure, and because propaganda for individual consumer goods is inevitably more effective than the (nonexistent) propaganda in favor of social consumption would be, the capitalist monopolies play a preponderant role in the orientation of all aspects of societal life, impose their own style and their own consumption structure on society, and demagogically challenge the legitimacy of social consumption.

Indeed, the entire sphere of *potentially creative needs* is sacrificed, abandoned, and subordinated to the capitalist sector. In other words, human needs are subordinated to the exigencies of

[3] It may, however, have a *political* or *calculated* interest in satisfying these needs, and this is the distinguishing characteristic of neo-capitalism. The development and democratization of education, for example, are necessary for the continuance of monopolist expansion; and the improvement of public health helps to create a more efficient labor force. Nevertheless, this interest is calculated and not spontaneous, because the growth of the social sector, by increasing fiscal pressure and by at least potentially restricting the domain of private initiative, intensifies the contradiction between the social character of production and the private appropriation of its means and results.

[4] Whether these capitalists are individuals or corporate bodies makes little difference insofar as their consumption, investment, or reinvestment practices are concerned.

capital, consumption is subordinated to production conceived as an end in itself, and the qualitative development of individuals and of their social relationships is subordinated to the quantitative development of accumulation.

The social and historical circumstances which permit this type of subordination are essentially those of alienated labor in highly industrialized societies. By this I mean that the type of passive consumer needed by monopoly capitalism in order to extend its control into all spheres of civil life and to shape them in its image—this type of "alienated consumer" is nothing more than an individual who reflects in his consumer needs his alienation as agent of production: he is the "atomized" worker, made passive by his pre-set monotonous tasks, subjected at the same time to military discipline and to the gentle constraint of neo-paternalism, without responsibility in his work, without power over the purposes of his production, cut off from his product, condemned to sell his time, and reduced and encouraged to *dream* that he is a human being (because he cannot be human in reality) by the appropriation of prefabricated symbols of humanity, by the consumption of pseudo-culture and escape.

Thus labor struggles would indirectly and involuntarily tend to play into the hands of monopoly capitalism if they limited themselves to demands for greater consumption, and if they did not at the same time demand power and control, challenging the work situation, the organization of production, the model and the structures of consumption: in short, if they did not challenge the purposes of societal work and capitalist civilization itself.

In this regard it is important to demonstrate that "affluence" and exploitation are two sides of the same reality, because capitalist accumulation necessarily engenders waste. Capitalism tends to incorporate in its consumer goods a maximum of "added value" (that is to say, source of profit), *whether this increases the use value of the product or not*—as, for example, when it complicates the satisfaction of simple needs by luxurious wrappings and ornamentation, by the production of costly replacement goods which soon supplant their less expensive counterparts, or by the substitution of durable articles which can be produced in great quantity by already amortized fixed capital with goods which wear out more rapidly (new synthetic textiles, for example) which make new investment necessary and allow the capitalist to avoid competition and to maintain his prices and his profit rate at a high level.

The answer is obviously not to call for "austerity" in the name of some idealist or puritan distinction between "true and healthy" versus "artificial and decadent" needs. Instead it must be remembered that in economies where productive resources remain scarce one cannot produce everything at the same time, one must establish an order of priorities. And the order of priorities inherent in capitalism means that priority goes to individual products for "affluent" consumption, products which permit a high profit rate, accompanied by over-exploitation and a long workweek, to the detriment of the social satisfaction of cultural and social needs, at the sacrifice of individual and collective autonomy and of their full human development. To subordinate production to consumption, to subordinate the economy to needs and to bring it under the control of the producers on all the levels where these needs appear and where this control can be exercised (company, community, city, region, industry, nation, school) is the most general objective of anti-monopolist planning; and this objective cannot be attained unless a reversal of the balance of power on all levels breaks the de facto dictatorship of capital.

2. *The Internationalization of the Struggle*

Economic planning is not an end in itself. Against certain reformist theorists of the labor movement we must reemphasize that economic planning is of interest to the working class only insofar as it permits them to increase their powers, to assert their candidacy as ruling class, and to take the control of the economy out of the hands of the direct and indirect representatives of monopoly capital, because those are the preconditions both for the satisfaction of social needs and for the establishment of a democracy which is open to socialism.

Similarly, planning cannot be limited to a simple redistribution of income and to the achievement of certain social objectives, in exchange for the working class's collaboration with the Plan—

that is to say "wage discipline" and abandonment of class autonomy and of the demand for power. Planning interests the working class because it permits a great public debate about the objectives of the economy and its order of priorities and therefore allows the working class to present alternative solutions, a different model of development—to show that the problems and the obstacles in the way of optimum solutions stem not from material causes but from the political character of capitalism. "And where can this new hierarchy of consumption come from, if not from the struggles of the working class, struggles to achieve a wage level which is independent of the vicissitudes of the production cycle, struggles for jobs which make full utilization of the cultural and professional capacities of the worker? The rejection of this autonomy would mean only one thing: it would turn the discussion of priorities into a vague exchange of moral platitudes, and in fact it would create a program whose every mechanism reinforces and crystallizes precisely the hierarchy of consumption and the shaping of consumption by production that we are complaining about." [5]

It is therefore out of the question, when we speak of the working class's "intervening" in the planning process and of the goals and alternative solutions which it presents on that occasion, to make the working class "participate" in the elaboration of the Plan in order then to hold it prisoner of the compromises forced on it under cover of technical arbitration and social peace by a committee of "apolitical" experts.

But it is also impossible to take up an extremist position of "all or nothing," of refusing to fight for partial solutions and for feasible structural reforms, on the pretext that these would not abolish capitalism. It is impossible to restrict oneself to organizing all discontents while waiting for the day when the working class will take power. Quite the contrary, the will and the chance to seize power will not become real unless the working class movement is able to outline concrete alternative solutions, solutions founded on the workers' needs, which are already compatible with

[5] Luciano Barca, Report to the *Gramsci Institute's Symposium on Economic Planning*, 1963.

the potentials of the economy but evidently not compatible with existing economic, social, and political structures.[6]

While fighting for these alternative solutions and for the structural reforms they require, the working class movement must be able to establish *continuity* between the objectives of present mass struggles and the prospect of a socialist transformation of society. The movement must be able to make the workers, on all levels of their existence, feel that socialist society is not located beyond the present-day society; and that it is not capable of halting or even reversing the processes that are under way and that threaten the vested interest of pre-capitalist classes or strata. Rather, socialist society exists within these processes as their internal contradiction, as both the objective and subjective necessity to go beyond them toward new objectives.

In this way the "antagonistic participation" of the working class in the elaboration of the Plan and in the definition of its objectives becomes an occasion for great public confrontations which make it possible to mobilize the working classes for intermediate, structural objectives, to raise their level of consciousness, to demonstrate and to increase their militancy and their power.

In practice, compromises may nevertheless have to be accepted. But:

1. The compromise will be understood explicitly for what it is: the provisional result of the temporary relationship of forces, to be modified and altered by future battles;

2. The compromise will be more favorable to the working

[6] Structural reforms should not be conceived as measures granted by the bourgeois State at the end of a compromise negotiated with it, measures which leave its power intact. They should rather be considered as cracks created in the system by attacks on its weak points. The distinguishing characteristic of such a strategy is that it aims by means of partial victories to shake the system's equilibrium profoundly, to sharpen its contradictions, to intensify its crisis, and, by a succession of attacks and counterattacks, to raise the class struggle to a greater intensity, at a higher and higher level. To fight for alternative solutions and for structural reforms (that is to say, for intermediate objectives) is not to fight for improvements in the capitalist system; it is rather to break it up, to restrict it, to create counter-powers which, instead of creating a new equilibrium, undermine its very foundations.

class, will better strengthen it and lead to more fruitful future battles because the working class will have exercised vigorous pressure during the discussion phase, thus destroying the myth of the Plan "as a scientific reality determined by objective necessity."

It is clear that this strategic and dialectic utilization of planning for the purpose of constantly raising the level of labor struggle is not compatible with the bureaucratic definition of abstract objectives. The workers' organizations cannot work out, at the summit, a more or less rigid alternative schema of international specialization on the Common Market level; or else the dialectic of the struggle will be bogged down and the organizations cut off from the masses.

Nor can they ignore the problems of coherence and of international coordination of their objectives and programs. In particular they cannot work toward national solutions whose adoption would push the burden of a given crisis onto the shoulders of the working class of a neighboring country. They cannot fight the international strategies of the monopolies, holding companies, and manufacturers' organizations with narrowly national struggles, or they will sharpen their internal divisions and weaken each other.

We therefore return to the problem of the working class's international strategy to meet European integration and eventual supranational planning. For even local struggles for concrete and immediate objectives must be coordinated, must fit into an international strategy, in order to be effective. It is easy to illustrate this statement by some examples:

1. In industries which are clearly overcrowded, where vigorous commercial competition is the rule (the automobile industry for example), every domestic oligopoly answers the workers' demands by pointing to the necessity for remaining on a competitive footing with the other oligopolies. The management of Renault, argued successfully that if it gave in to labor pressure, its investment plan, its production cost and selling price, and its ability to compete with foreign manufacturers would be threatened, and therefore the workers' jobs would be threatened too, and thus it

would be in the general interest for the workers not to limit management's freedom of action.

The working class cannot avoid being forced to shoulder the burden of oligopolist competition unless it can both answer management's arguments with a detailed and precise comparison of labor costs, working hours, and fringe benefits in other countries (the systematic exchange of information between the different labor federations is therefore indispensable); and coordinate its demands, especially in the case of contract renewal negotiations. Only in this way is it possible to avoid the eventuality that labor victories in one country, relating to wages, hours, vacations, and restrictions on the profit rate, may be exploited by the manufacturers of another country in order to take over a part of the former's market. In this way the present tendency of industry-wide contracts to be most favorable to management will be reversed.

It is also possible to perfect a "leapfrog" tactic, in which the labor movement of each country fights for the advantages won by the labor movement of another country, so that each labor movement spurs on the other movements because one of them will always be ahead of the others in the advantages it has won relating to one or another aspect of the work situation. The coordination of labor demands does not in effect imply their perfect identity. On the contrary, heterogeneity should be maintained as a source of perpetual ferment and agitation.

2. In an industry which is dominated by an international monopoly (for example, Phillips and IBM in electronics, Frigidaire in household appliances, Lever and Nestlé in the food industry, Saint-Gobain in the glass industry, Olivetti or Remington in office equipment), by an international cartel (oil and petro-chemicals, aluminum), or by an international holding company, local strikes will lose their effectiveness as weapons once the different national markets have become integrated, especially when production surpluses have clearly appeared. Like Remington, which closed its factory in Caluire because factories in Germany, Italy, and Holland were more profitable, any other trust or holding company

will tend to answer a strike in a single one of its subsidiaries or companies with an indefinite lockout if the workers who produce identical or comparable goods in other countries stay on their jobs. In all industrial sectors which operate essentially on the international level, the coordination of labor struggles must necessarily take the form of synchronization, of *joint action!*

3. In industries which are experiencing structural crises (coal mining, shipbuilding, and partly the textile industry), the elaboration of alternative or reorientation plans must take account of the position of these industries within the entire Common Market and of their markets on a world-wide scale. The struggle against layoffs in the shipbuilding industry, for example, must be accompanied on the one hand by demands based on the nature and scope of the production which could be achieved except for the bankruptcy of the owners, taking into account the world market (socialist countries included), and on the other hand, by demands concerning the manufacture of different items (heavy and light machinery, for example) which the shipyards could undertake if they were reconverted at public initiative, taking into account the needs of the underdeveloped countries.

The labor movement cannot carry out an offensive strategy in the matter of industrial and regional reconversion unless it makes use of Common Market-wide economic studies of each industry, a strategy which presupposes a constant exchange of information between the economic research departments of all the national labor federations.

The lesson to be drawn from these three examples is that the working class movement is forced to internationalize its strategy at least to the degree to which capitalism has internationalized its own. And this brings us back to the questions which we raised at the beginning of this chapter: because the factual internationalization of markets, of production, and of fiscal policies tends toward the creation of supranational planning and a supranational State, what should be the working class attitude toward these institutions? Should it condemn them, or should it participate in their establishment, hoping thereby to make them more democratic?

Or should it wait until they are established before defining its tactics?

The first of these attitudes would be sterile: the condemnation of a process which is already under way necessarily remains on the level of abstract verbiage and can supply neither the basis nor the opening of a strategy.

The second attitude, participation, would be a fool's bargain under present circumstances. What is there, in effect, for the working class to participate in? If the supranational centers of decision making of the EEC were subject to democratic control by representative assemblies which could influence its policy and mobilize the masses around alternative perspectives, then, of course, participation would make sense. But that is not the case at all. The EEC is nothing more than the technocratic emanation of States in which the working class holds no power whatsoever, and it is free from all control by representative assemblies. To participate in the definition of a supranational policy under these conditions would be, for the working class, to cut itself off from the masses by entering into a confidential relationship with technocracy and the representatives of big business; it would be to agree to fight without weapons against fully armed adversaries, to accept predetermined structures which would then be impossible to challenge. It would be difficult to believe that the labor movement could achieve on the supranational level a degree of influence and of power which it does not possess on the national level.

But the third alternative, that of sitting back and waiting, is not possible either. If the labor movement waits for supranational bodies with real power to define the economic, social, financial, fiscal, and monetary policies and structures of each country, it will be too late: it will be forced into the defensive. And it will have wasted the interim period in which it could have worked toward the creation of an international labor front and the outline of an alternative perspective.

Because that, above all, is what must be achieved: a front which by means of converging national pressures can play the role of a real counter-power on the international level.

The orientation and content of these pressures have already been discussed above and can be summarized as follows:

1. Defense of jobs, of occupational autonomy, and of company autonomy, which implies workers' control over the local and international policies of the company, a control which in the case of cartels or monopolies operating on an international level can be achieved only by the international confrontation and coordination of the problems faced by all the unions in the given industry and of the actions which they undertake. The strengthening or the achievement of workers' power within the companies is a primary objective.

2. A reconversion and development policy corresponding to the needs and the equilibrium of each region, which presupposes:

a) the decentralization and the democratization of economic power centers, because an eventual "European" regional reconversion and development policy must result from the harmonization of decentralized projects, and should not proceed according to the contrary direction, as is happening at present; and

b) the development of public initiative both in expanding industrial sectors and in the sphere of regional and agricultural development. The defense of nationalization, the struggle to extend nationalizations and to submit them to democratic control, is a second imperative.

3. The reorientation of the economy and of the consumption structure according to real priorities, which presupposes:

a) the development of labor struggles for higher wages and better working conditions, and the uncompromising defense of union autonomy;

b) the struggle for fiscal, social, and investment policies which are qualitatively and quantitatively different from capitalist "planning";

c) the socialization of the investment function (the effective nationalization of credit) which, supported by the local workers' power over company policies, is the fundamental precondition of anti-monopolist planning.

During the interim period preceding the establishment of supranational powers, converging pressures toward these objectives—objectives which no European labor movement can take exception to—can exercise a decisive influence on the policy of the EEC. These pressures can be exercised both on the national and the supranational levels.

In the present phase the working class movement can make its weight felt most effectively in the EEC and can best influence the EEC to become compatible, or at least not incompatible, with new democratic victories which further socialism by concentrating its action on the different national governments. Because if under labor pressure a given State is forced to make concessions or to undertake structural transformations, it will also be forced to fight within the EEC to ensure that the policy which has been imposed on it, whether it is compatible with the Treaty of Rome or not, does not remain a national peculiarity; and at that moment it will be up to the labor movements of the other countries to force their respective governments in the same direction, to prevent an anti-capitalist victory in one country being counteracted or exploited to the workers' detriment by neighboring capitalist States.

But in a later, probably not too distant phase, when the national governments will have been largely dispossessed of their economic powers by the EEC, the workers' (as well as the farmers') organizations must be in a position to exercise their pressures on the latter; it is on the supranational level that these organizations must challenge the big economic decisions made by the "planners," must propose anti-monopolist counter-decisions, must prevent the EEC from becoming an apparatus of economic war against anti-imperialist revolutions or against the socialist countries, an apparatus which precludes all prospects of the socialist integration of Europe.

This action on the supranational level presupposes that the different labor organizations within the EEC possess a common strategy and political plans; a condition which cannot at present be achieved and will be unattainable for quite some time. To the degree that summit agreements among labor organizations would tend to contain only a "minimum program," they are not even desirable.

But what can be achieved at present is an international inter-union council, for the purposes of influencing the various bodies of the EEC more specifically, and of preventing any supranational decisions, legislations, or institutions incompatible with the above-cited objectives, namely: (a) with the achievement of workers' power in the companies; (b) with the democratization of economic decisions, the strengthening of public initiative and the expansion of nationalization; (c) with union autonomy and with the socialization of the investment function.

Another thing which can be done at present is for each labor movement to begin work on a series of thorough studies concerning national objectives in regional development questions, social priorities (education, social security, public services, wage standardization, paid holidays, etc.), full employment and union powers, as well as studies of reconversion.

The coordination of objectives and action will arise out of the confrontation of these studies as a practical necessity, in somewhat the same way as European "planning" arises out of the confrontation of different business programs. Each labor movement, informed about the objectives of the others, will be led to take account of them in its own plans. The elements of a joint economic development plan on the European level will thus be created, and the necessity of working out such a plan, of opposing such a plan to that of the cartels and of the EEC will become clear as soon as such a plan becomes possible.

All this in no way implies that one should at this time work toward the unification and the centralization of labor strategy. Such measures, besides being impossible at present, would only result in bureaucratic sclerosis. What must be done instead is to coordinate the various sectoral, regional, or national strategies so that they complement, not counteract each other. The conditions which make anti-capitalist breakthroughs possible in each country must be preserved throughout the EEC, while at the same time letting each separate struggle develop according to its particular qualities, in following their own methods and their own specific objectives, even if the latter are more advanced than the objectives of other labor movements. In no case should the brakes be applied to a given national or sectoral struggle on the pretext that it is too far ahead of the struggles of other countries. On the contrary, one must trust in the contagious effect of each national victory, because *national* victories will not be possible much longer, but it is from them that the labor movement principally draws its strength.

It should nevertheless and from now on begin to train itself in joint actions, no matter how decentralized or how limited their objectives may be. Only by united action will the movement be able in the future—when the nature and the orientation of supranational powers are at stake—to constitute itself in a front which is able to weigh more heavily than the trusts on the policies of the national governments and on European institutions. And this unity of action in turn will be possible only if the workers' organizations uncompromisingly defend their autonomy, and if they reject all forms of subordination to the policies of States as well as to the policies of political parties.

"Throughout Europe," Vittorio Foa writes, "the labor movement today faces the most serious problem of its history. The problem does not consist of a brutal attack by the forces of reaction. The problem is rather the tendency to subordinate the unions to the so-called "incomes" policy, that is to say the governmental planning of wages, a plan which the unions are asked to accept in the name of the best interests of the nation. Now, to accept a pre-set annual rate of wage increases would mean to abandon all labor autonomy at the scene of production, to endorse the present developmental mechanism as the permanent guiding law of the union.

"The very existence of the European labor movement is at stake, in its substance if not in its form. The closer and closer links between governmental policy and big business, as well as the spread of State capitalism, raise the question of the relationships between labor unions and political parties to the head of the agenda. A situation of labor unity founded on agreements between political parties would force the unions into the opposition—or into collaboration with the government, depending on the changing political situation—if indeed it did not also create schisms and divisions in the labor movement. It is on this field that the European labor movement must today prove its autonomy and its ability to establish labor unity beyond national boundaries." [7]

[7] "I socialisti e il sindacato," *Problemi del Socialismo*, June 1963.

APPENDIX

French and Italian Trade Unions

1. *France*

CGT—*Confédération Générale du Travail* (General Confederation of Labor). Largest of the trade union federation, with a membership of about 45 per cent of the approximately 12 million organized workers. Its leadership is largely Communist or radical left. Since its establishment in 1895, the organization split three times (1922, 1939, and 1947) over the question whether union policy should be subordinate to or independent of political parties, specifically the French Communist party.

CGT-FO—*Confédération Générale du Travail*, "Force Ouvrière" (General Confederation of Labor, Working Force). Usually referred to as *Force Ouvrière*, this group split off from the CGT in 1947. It is social-democratic in outlook and comprises about 15 per cent of the total union membership.

CGTC—*Confédération Française de Travailleurs Chrétiens* (French Confederation of Christian Workers). Founded in 1919 as a Catholic trade union, committed to the principles laid down in the papal encyclical *Rerum Novarum*, this group has gradually loosened its ties with the Catholic Church. Leftist Catholics and independent socialists occupy the leading positions in the organization, which has a membership of approximately 21 per cent of the total union membership.

CGC—*Confédération Générale des Cadres* (General Confederation of Senior Employees). Founded in 1945 by technicians in industry who were unwilling to submit to the rule of a workers' majority in both CGT and CFTC, it stands between the employers' organizations and the trade unions.

2. *Italy*

CGIL—*Confederazione Generale Italiana del Lavoro* (Italian General Confederation of Labor). Largest of the Italian trade union federations, with approximately 46 per cent of the total union membership of about 6 million. Established in June 1944 as a unified democratic national federation of labor, its founders hoped to transcend political division. However, in 1948, the Christian Democrats decided to leave and form their own organization; and in 1949 the Social Democrats and Republicans withdrew. Socialists and Communists have a controlling voice in the organization. In recent years, union policy has tended to be more radical than party policy.

CISL—*Confederazione Italiana Sindacati dei Lavoratori* (Italian Confederation of Workers' Unions). Formed in 1950 by Christian Democratic, Social Democratic, and Republican union leaders who left CGIL, and attempted, with government support, to break the latter's hold on the factory floors. In recent years, the CISL Metal-workers Union has developed into a radical and anti-governmental force whose Catholic leaders work in close cooperation with the CGIL metal workers. The membership is approximately 40 per cent of the total union membership.

UIL—*Unione Italiana del Lavoro* (Italian Union of Labor). Established in 1950 by disparate elements, mostly Republicans, Social Democrats, and some neo-Fascists, it views itself as a third force between the two large federations. Anti-Communist in orientation, it sympathizes with the American trade unions. The membership is about 11 per cent of the total union membership.

In addition to the three main labor federations, there exist a number of independent unions and one neo-Fascist labor organization, CISNAL—*Confederazione Italiana Sindacati Nazionali Lavoratori* (Italian Confederation of National Workers' Unions). Their combined membership is reported to be below 500,000, and their influence negligible.

For further information, see

Le Syndicalisme en France, by George Lafranc, Collection

"Que Sais-je?", Paris: Presses Universitaires de France (1964).

The Italian Labor Movement: Problems and Prospects, by Joseph La Palombara, Ithaca: Cornell University Press (1957).

Index